FOR YOUR PROFESSIONAL BOOKSHELF

from

ENERGY PSYCHOLOGY PRESS

The Human Hologram
Living Your Life in Harmony with the Unified Field
By Dr. Robin Kelly

A London-trained physician presents evidence that our physical bodies are perpetually being formed upon an invisible field of information, and that as our consciousness interacts with that field, we can optimize our health.

Softcover, 6" x 9", 256 pages $16.95

Soul Medicine
Awakening Your Inner Blueprint for Abundant Health and Energy
By Norman Shealy, MD, PhD, and Dawson Church, PhD

A neurosurgeon and founder of the American Holistic Medical Association, Shealy teams up with health researcher Dawson Church to present the latest studies showing the healing effects of energy, intention and consciousness.

Softcover, 6" x 9", 296 pages $17.95

Heal Your Mind, Rewire Your Brain
Applying the Exciting New Science of Brain Plasticity for Creativity, Peace and Presence
By Patt Lind-Kyle, MA

Applies the latest exciting scientific discoveries in a practical, step-by-step program that literally rewires neural connections in the brain for greater happiness.

Hardcover, 6" x 9", 32 Illustrations, 253 pages $26.95

Creating Healing Relationships
Professional Standards for Energy Therapy Practitioners
By Dorothea Hover-Kramer, EdD, RN, DCEP

Written by the co-founder of ACEP, the professional organization for Energy Psychology, this is the first book to seriously address the need for professional standards in the rapidly growing field of energy healing.

Hardcover, 6" x 9", 256 pages $35

Body Eloquence
The Power of Myth and Story to Awaken the Body's Energies
By Nancy Mellon, MFT with Ashley Ramsden

Have you ever had an ache or pain, and wished your body could talk to you and tell you what was wrong? Drawing from mythology, medicine, biology and energetic healing, this book shows the messages that our organs are communicating to us.

Trade Paper, 7" x 10", 15 Illustrations, 260 pages $18.95

Energy Healer's Ethics Handbook
By David Feinstein, PhD, with Donna Eden

This comprehensive, case-oriented guide allows veterans of the field and newcomers alike to work through a wide range of ethical dilemmas before they arise, helping you to prevent professional errors that could hurt you, your clients, and your practice.

Hardcover, 6" x 9", 210 pages $39

ENERGY PSYCHOLOGY PRESS

Order now at EnergyPsychologyPress.com

Energy Psychology
Theory, Research, and Treatment

A Journal of the National Institute for Integrative Healthcare (NIIH.org)

www.EnergyPsychologyJournal.org

Energy Psychology: Theory, Research, and Treatment is a peer-reviewed professional journal dedicated to reporting developments in the field of energy psychology (EP) that are of interest to health care professionals and researchers. It contains original empirical research into the efficacy of EP methods; theoretical, experimental, and basic science papers illuminating the mechanisms of action of EP; clinical insights on the application of EP to various populations, and interfaces with other interventions; book reviews, and abstracts published in other journals that are of relevance to the EP field. Its goal is to further the development of EP as an evidence-based method in the healing sciences. It conforms to the editorial, stylistic, and ethical standards of the American Psychological Association (APA.org).

Energy Psychology: Theory, Research, and Treatment (ISSN 1949-6575) is published biannually (November and May) by Energy Psychology Press, PO Box 442, Fulton, CA 95439. For customer service or advertising information, contact 707-237-6951 or energypsychologypress@gmail.com.

POSTMASTER: Send address changes to: *Energy Psychology* journal, PO Box 442, Fulton, CA 95439.

YEARLY SUBSCRIPTION RATES: $49.95 per issue, $99.95 per year.

AUTHOR ENQUIRIES: Submit paper copies of proposed papers to *Energy Psychology* journal, PO Box 442, Fulton, CA 95439. Include an e-mail address and phone number for the corresponding author. All submissions should conform fully to the requirements of the *Publication Manual of the American Psychological Association,* sixth edition. Include a cover letter as specified on the "Submissions" link at www.EnergyPsychologyJournal.org, and manuscripts should be prepared in conformity with the other standards published there. Acceptance or rejection will be made via e-mail; paper copies will not be returned. If a submission is accepted for peer review, all subsequent contact will occur via e-mail. Deadline for Spring issue submissions is Jan 15 of each year, and July 15 for Fall issue.

REPRINTS: Back issues are available for $49.95. Reprint ordering information may be found at www.EnergyPsychologyPress.com. To order 100 or more copies of a particular paper, contact energypsychologypress@gmail.com.

DISCLAIMERS:

Contents

May 2021 • Volume 13, Number 1

About

ENERGY PSYCHOLOGY: THEORY, RESEARCH, AND TREATMENT

Energy Psychology (EP) is an evolving and maturing field that is rapidly meeting the standards of proof for "evidence-based" practice. Studies of EP have demonstrated its efficacy for a wide range of psychological and physical problems, from phobias to pain to posttraumatic stress disorder. EP is now being researched in hospital systems such as Britain's National Health Service (NHS), large private hospital chains such as Kaiser Permanente and Sutter Health, and the United States Department of Veterans Affairs (VA). By providing a rigorous, high-quality, peer-reviewed platform for the publication of research results, theory, and clinical insights, this journal provides a forum for the exchange of the key discoveries and ideas that drive the EP field forward.

—Dawson Church, PhD
Editor, *Energy Psychology: Theory, Research, and Treatment*

The journal publishes work in the following areas:

EDITORIAL ESSAYS include guest editorials from some of the best thinkers and researchers in EP today;

ORIGINAL RESEARCH provides empirical evidence for various EP methods;

CLINICAL REPORTS describe the use of EP with challenging conditions and specific populations and provide guidance for empirical research;

INTERFACES WITH OTHER THERAPIES show how EP is typically used in conjunction with other methods, such as cognitive behavior therapy (CBT), mindfulness therapy, addiction counseling, sports psychology, medicine, energy medicine, meditation, and life coaching;

REVIEW ARTICLES are theoretical papers, literature reviews, reports of innovations, and analyses that explore issues from the professional condition of EP to the physiological mechanisms of action of EP;

BOOK REVIEWS cover new and classic EP-related titles;

ABSTRACTS published in other journals relevant to EP are reprinted.

EDITORIAL BOARD

Alzheimer's Is Associated with Repetitive Negative Thinking

Dawson Church

Today we take the images from EEGs and MRIs for granted. They are a fundamental part of medical diagnosis and treatment. Yet the EEG is less than a century old and the MRI less than half that age. Before visionary scientists developed these technologies, the workings of the brain were deduced from the behavioral characteristics of patients with brain damage. When German doctor Hans Berger began to share his first EEG recordings in the 1930s, academic neuroscientists ridiculed his findings. Depressed and shunned, he committed suicide in 1941 (Tudor et al., 2005).

The technology eventually caught on, however, and has been developed to a remarkable degree. Think about how the screen of your current phone has a much higher resolution than the one you were using five years back. Similar technological breakthroughs have recently occurred with brain imaging machines. The latest models can track the activity of a single neuron.

Over the course of four years, researchers at University College London used the newest PET scanning technology to track the brains of 292 people aged 55 years and older (Marchant et al., 2020). The study measured the accumulation of two proteins in their brains. These molecules, beta amyloid and tau, are markers of Alzheimer's disease. They stick together to form gummy "plaques." These interfere with neural signaling, much the way gunk builds up in the plumbing under your sink, eventually stopping the flow.

Before the development of advanced PET scanners, the only way to measure the accumulation of tau and beta amyloid plaques was by sampling brain tissue, usually after death. Studies measuring behavioral traits in living people and comparing them to plaque deposits were not possible. Technological advances continue to make entirely new forms of research possible.

Science used to believe that Alzheimer's is a "purely genetic" disease. A signaling gene called APOE is key. It comes in three flavors: APOE2, E3, and E4. People with APOE2 have very low risk of Alzheimer's. Those with two E4 genes, one from each parent, have an Alzheimer's risk over 90%.

The University College researchers looked at cognitive functions such as attention span and memory in their subjects. Over the course of four years, they noted which people had a faster accumulation of plaques and compared this with a host of lifestyle and psychological factors.

What had the strongest correlation with the buildup of beta and tau proteins? It wasn't the presence of the APOE4 gene or anything to do with the participants' lifestyle. The single factor with the greatest correlation was negative thinking—specifically, repetitive negative thinking (RNT). A habit of RNT meant a higher risk of Alzheimer's. Not only that, but the relationship between them scaled. The more RNT the faster the buildup of plaque.

Lead author Dr. Natalie Marchant commented that "depression and anxiety in midlife and old age are already known to be risk factors for dementia. Here we found that certain thinking patterns implicated in depression and anxiety could be an unlined reason why people with those disorders are more likely to develop dementia. Taken alongside other studies which link depression and anxiety with dementia risk, we expect that chronic negative thinking patterns over a long period of time could increase the risk of dementia."

Negative thinking behaviors included rumination about the past and worry about the future.

Neurologist Dr. Richard Isaacson, founder of the Alzheimer's prevention clinic at New York Presbyterian Hospital, noted that "this is the first study showing a biological relationship between RNT and Alzheimer's pathology. Many people at risk are unaware about the specific negative impact of worrying and rumination directly on the brain."

The researchers speculated about practices that might promote positive thinking. They plan a further study to test the possibility that meditation might reverse the process. Existing studies show that the more positive we are the lower our risk of death from strokes and heart attacks.

Millions of people, me included, are now getting genetic tests from companies like 23 and Me. They give you an impressive report showing your genetic risk for common diseases like Alzheimer's, diabetes, cancer, and heart attacks. Yet they make zero allowance for consciousness. They fail to recognize that the way we use our minds influences the activation of those genes.

You can train your brain using positive emotional states, just like training a muscle. One study found that meditating for just 12 minutes a day produced measurable positive changes in brain anatomy in eight weeks (Church, 2020). Gratitude has the same effect. So do happiness, compassion, and altruism.

These studies show that even "purely genetic" diseases are influenced by consciousness.

Consciousness may be our most underutilized asset. Many people allow themselves an infinite diet of RNT, unaware of the damage it may do to their brains.

Using your superpower of consciousness deliberately, you can direct your attention in healthy and uplifting ways. Choose positivity and you shape your brain and direct your gene expression. That's a superpower that every human being possesses.

References

Church, D. (2020). *Bliss brain: The neuroscience of remodeling your brain for resilience, creativity, and joy.* Carlsbad, CA: Hay House.

Marchant, N. L., Lovland, L. R., Jones, R., Pichet Binette, A., Gonneaud, J., Arenaza-Urquijo, E. M., ... PREVENT-AD Research Group. (2020). Repetitive negative thinking is associated with amyloid, tau, and cognitive decline. *Alzheimer's and Dementia, 16*(7), 1054–1064.

Tudor, M., Tudor, L., & Tudor, K. I. (2005). Hans Berger (1873–1941) and the history of electroencephalography. *Acta Medica Croatica, 59*(4), 307–313.

CLINICAL REPORT

Trauma-Based Energy Psychology Treatment Is Associated with Client Rehabilitation at an Addiction Clinic

Adriana Popescu, Avery Lane for Women, Novato, California, USA

Abstract

Energy Psychology (EP) comprises a set of innovative and powerful techniques that can be used to enhance treatment progress and outcomes for addiction and co-occurring disorders, particularly posttraumatic stress disorder (PTSD). This article identifies the limitations of the current addiction treatment paradigm and presents a variety of ways in which one dual diagnosis treatment program for women addresses these limitations with the EP approach. Research on EP and its mechanism of action is presented, along with specific examples of how the tools are used at the treatment facility, case studies, client and therapist feedback, treatment guidelines, and outcome data. Data for 123 clients in the program collected over a 3.5-year period include reductions in mental health symptomology during treatment as follows: depression scores from 79% at intake to 16% at last survey, $p < .001$; anxiety scores from 73% to 8%, $p < .001$; trauma symptoms from 76% to 30%, $p < .001$; suicidality from 53% to 11%, $p < .001$; binge eating from 33% to 11%, $p = .01$; and compensatory eating disorder behaviors from 41% to 11%, $p = .074$. The evidence presented indicates that EP can be a very empowering and effective adjunct to treatment for co-occurring disorders, particularly for emotional self-regulation, cognitive restructuring, and trauma processing. The data and clinical results from Avery Lane are consistent with those derived from meta-analyses, clinical trials, and experiences at other treatment centers. This body of literature demonstrates that EP is a powerful, evidence-based approach that sets the standard for effective addiction treatment.

Keywords: addiction, dual diagnosis, trauma, PTSD, depression, anxiety, Energy Psychology, Emotional Freedom Techniques, EFT

Adriana Popescu, PhD, is a licensed clinical psychologist in private practice and the clinical director at Avery Lane for Women, an innovative treatment program for women with co-occurring addiction and mental health disorders. She is coauthor of the *Conscious Being Workbook* and *The Conscious Recovery Method Workbook.* **Correspondence:** Adriana Popescu, PhD, 505A San Marin Drive #300, Novato, CA 94945; email: apopescu@averylaneforwomen.com. **Disclosure:** The author conducts trainings and provides clinical services with the approaches examined in this paper.

Substance use and mental health disorders continue to be a largely underdiagnosed and undertreated health issue in the United States. According to the Substance Abuse and Mental Health Services Administration (SAMHSA, 2020), in 2019, 20.6% (51.5 million) of all adults aged 18 and older in the U.S. were living with a mental illness. Of those, only about 44.8% (23 million) received mental health services in the previous year.

Furthermore, the National Institute on Drug Abuse (NIDA, 2020) reports that multiple national population surveys have found that about half of those who experience a mental illness during their lifetime will also experience a substance use disorder and vice versa (Santucci, 2012). This is referred to as dual diagnosis, or co-occurring disorders.

The statistics for those with co-occurring mental health and substance use disorders are discouraging. According to one study, of the 20.3 million people in the United States with substance use disorders, 37.9% also had mental disorders, and of the 41.1 million people with mental health disorders, 18.2% also had substance use disorders. For those people who needed treatment, 52.5%

received neither substance use treatment nor mental health treatment, 34.5% received mental health treatment only, 3.9% received substance use treatment only, and only 9.1% received both substance use and mental health treatment (Han et al., 2017).

Research indicates that having co-occurring disorders not only impacts treatment accessibility, but also substance abuse treatment outcomes; clients with comorbid disorders demonstrate poorer treatment adherence (DeMarce et al., 2008) and higher rates of treatment dropout (Kelly & Daley, 2013; Torrens et al., 2012) than those without mental illness.

It is also important to note the impact of trauma in the course and outcome of dual diagnosis treatment. Many environmental influences are associated with an increased risk for both substance use disorders and mental illness including chronic stress, trauma, and adverse childhood experiences (NIDA, 2020). SAMHSA (2020) reports that of those who sought mental health treatment in 2019, 44.7% have experienced trauma and 41.9% meet the criteria for a diagnosis of posttraumatic stress disorder (PTSD). Those individuals who have experienced trauma are at much higher risk for drug use and substance use disorders, with poorer treatment outcomes (Berenz & Coffey, 2012).

Current Treatment Paradigm

The efficacy of traditional standards of care for addiction treatment has been disappointing. It has not proven to address adequately the complex needs of people with co-occurring substance use and mental health disorders. According to NIDA (2020), there is a need for comprehensive and integrated therapies to address comorbid disorders, and integrated treatments for co-occurring disorders have been found to be consistently superior compared with separate treatments for each diagnosis (DeMarce et al., 2008; Kelly & Daley, 2013; Torrens et al., 2012). Yet research indicates that only about 18% of substance use disorder treatment programs and 9% of mental health treatment programs in the U.S. actually have the capacity to serve this population in an integrated way (McGovern et al., 2014).

Traditional substance abuse treatment focuses primarily on the environmental causes of addiction and utilizes psychosocial interventions such as psychoeducation and peer support (e.g., 12-Step programs) to treat it. Mental health issues are often overlooked as there has been a longstanding bias against psychotropic medication, and many programs do not employ licensed mental health professionals who can provide psychotherapy or psychiatrists and nurses who can prescribe, dispense, and monitor medications (McGovern et al., 2014). Only more recently with the growing opioid epidemic and government mandates are more treatment programs incorporating biologically based approaches such as medication-assisted therapy (MAT).

This may in part explain why success rates for long-term sustained sobriety have been notoriously low in this treatment paradigm. In a meta-analysis of alcoholism treatment outcome studies, average short-term abstinence rates were only 43% for treated individuals (Monahan & Finney, 1996). Post-discharge relapse and eventual re-admission appear to be the norm, and the risk of relapse does not appear to abate until four to five years of abstinence (Dawson, 1996; De Soto et al., 1989; Vaillant, 1996). Retrospective and prospective treatment studies report that most clients undergo three to four episodes of care before reaching a stable state of abstinence (Anglin et al., 1997; Hser et al., 1997). Long-term abstinence rates at 10 years posttreatment increase to 57%, but so does the risk of mortality, with alcoholic participants being 9.5 times as likely to die as matched community controls over the follow-up period (Finney & Moos, 1991).

Another concern with the current treatment paradigm is the undertreatment of trauma and PTSD. The prevalence of PTSD is 1.4 to 5 times higher among individuals with co-occurring substance use disorders than those without (Cottler et al., 1992). Women are particularly impacted by trauma, with rates of physical or sexual abuse among treatment-seeking women with substance abuse ranging from 55% to 99%, and many of these women manifest trauma-related symptoms consistent with a diagnosis of PTSD (Najavits et al., 1997).

Trauma is often not treated in traditional substance abuse programs. While it may be identified as an underlying cause of addiction, the existing mindset has been not to process trauma in early recovery, but rather to wait until clients have at least six months to one year of sobriety. The challenge is that these clients are often unable to sustain sobriety for this long due to recurrent symptoms of trauma and PTSD such as flashbacks, hypervigilance, heightened anxiety, and a constant state of nervous system hyperarousal. People with PTSD often use substances in an attempt to quell their anxiety and to avoid dealing with trauma and its consequences (Boden et al., 2014).

Although when they are offered, the "standard of care" therapies for PTSD—cognitive processing therapy and prolonged exposure—are proving to be more effective than supportive talk therapy alone, a meta-review by Steenkamp et al. (2015) found that while many clients received some benefit, approximately two thirds retained their PTSD diagnosis after completing treatment.

Thus it appears that these traditional treatment programs are often not addressing all of what research suggests are the underlying causes of addiction and mental disorders, nor giving people adequate coping skills for managing and processing mental health symptoms and trauma. Energy Psychology (EP) offers an innovative and comprehensive approach that may address these limitations.

Energy Psychology

What is Energy Psychology? The professional organization for EP, the Association of Comprehensive Energy Psychology (ACEP, n.d.), provides the following explanation:

> Energy psychology (EP) comprises a family of methods designed to strategically and methodically intervene with human energy fields in elevating physical, mental, emotional and spiritual wellbeing. These approaches are used by practitioners of psychotherapy, counseling, coaching, energy healing, and health optimization.
>
> EP methods combine cognitive interventions (including focused awareness and imaginal exposure to traumatic memories) with stimulation of the human bio-energy systems such as meridians, chakras and the biofield. Activation of the bio-energy system during the intervention is thought to increase the speed and/or thoroughness of the work.
>
> Practitioners view issues as systemic, interactive bio-energetic patterns. This involves constant complex communication among neurobiological processes, electrophysiology, consciousness, and bioenergy systems (which may include the biofield, chakras, and meridians). Practitioners use a variety of demonstrated and self-applied techniques to help clients shift the flow of information and energy throughout these systems.
>
> Most EP approaches are active, focused and structured. EP approaches can be: 1) used as stand-alone interventions, 2) integrated within a broader clinical treatment or program of change or health optimization.

To facilitate change, EP methods integrate concepts and techniques from related fields, including psychological science, acupuncture meridian theory, neuroscience, physics/quantum mechanics, biology, medicine, and chiropractic. Since the 1970s, these methods have been further developed, refined, and supported via clinical experience and research across multiple areas of application.

In 1980, psychologist Roger Callahan effectively applied the principles of acupressure to psychotherapy with Thought Field Therapy (TFT; Callahan, 1985). In TFT, clients focus their attention on an upsetting situation while tapping their fingertips on a series of acupuncture points (acupoints) on the body. According to traditional Chinese medicine, from which acupuncture and acupressure are derived, this stimulation of acupoints releases the energetic blocks creating the problem being addressed, restoring a balance in the energy flow in the body that allows the psychological issue to be resolved in ways not possible while internal systems are stressed (Feinstein, 2018).

Callahan effectively applied these principles in his work with clients, many of whom struggled with anxiety disorders such as phobias and PTSD. With the success of Callahan's findings, he began to offer courses in TFT and his students went on to develop their own variations on TFT, including Gary Craig's Emotional Freedom Techniques (EFT; Craig & Fowlie, 1995), Larry Nims' Be Set Free Fast (BSFF; Nims & Sotkin, 2003), and numerous others. The method most frequently researched and utilized in clinical practice currently is EFT.

EP approaches have now been incorporated into a number of existing treatment paradigms. Schulz (2009) found that licensed mental health professionals working with childhood sexual abuse frequently combined EP with more traditional trauma treatment modalities, including cognitive behavioral therapy (CBT), Eye Movement Desensitization and Reprocessing

(EMDR), and solution-focused therapy. One therapist participant in the study remarked that "energy methods are ideal for sexual abuse survivors because there is less necessity to talk about, or relive, trauma. This lessens the possibility of re-traumatization" (p. 18).

EP has also been utilized in formal treatment programs such as the Warrior Combat Stress Reset Program (Reset), an intensive outpatient behavioral health program at the Carl R. Darnall Army Medical Center in Fort Hood, Texas. Here, active-duty soldiers with PTSD were successfully treated with EP in combination with trauma-focused behavioral health techniques and complementary and alternative medicine (CAM) modalities including acupuncture, massage, Reiki, reflexology, and yoga (Libretto et al., 2015).

Typical Treatment Protocol

In a typical tapping-based EP treatment session, the client thinks about a distressing event or memory, a negative or limiting belief, a difficult emotion, or an uncomfortable physical sensation such as pain or tension, while simultaneously tapping on a prescribed set of acupoints (Feinstein, 2018). This may also (in the case of EFT) include verbal cueing that pairs the negative stressor with positive affirmations, for example, "Even though I'm feeling this anxiety, I love and accept myself."

The intensity of distress is measured throughout the treatment by rating it from 0 to 10 on a Subjective Units of Distress (SUD) scale (Wolpe, 1968). With subsequent rounds (usually one to three minutes each) of tapping through the acupoints on various aspects of the stressor, the SUD level will decrease until a sense of calmness and neutrality is reached and no subjective distress is reported regarding that aspect of the problem.

In BSFF (Nims & Sotkin, 2003), another commonly used EP technique, the subconscious mind is instructed by a cue of the client's choosing to initiate a process of clearing the negative emotional roots of an upsetting issue or problem. The cue can be a word or phrase (such as "peace," relax," or "let it go"), a visual image (e.g., a calming scene in nature), or a physical gesture (e.g., a hand on the heart). The SUD scale is used to measure the level of distress in the same way as in EFT. The client uses the cue for all thoughts, beliefs, emotions, and physical sensations that are creating distress until the SUD level decreases and a sense of calm and neutrality is achieved.

Brainspotting (BSP; Grand, 2013) derives from EMDR (Shapiro, 1995), a psychotherapy treatment that was originally designed to alleviate the distress associated with traumatic memories. BSP works by using specific eye positions to access, process, and release the core neurophysiological sources of physical or emotional pain, trauma, dissociation, and a variety of other symptoms. Left and right brain stimulation is enhanced with Biolateral sound delivered through earphones. In a typical session, the client focuses on the somatosensory experience of the symptom or problem, and a specific eye position is located (the "brainspot") that most activates the distress. The client fixes their gaze on that brainspot and this stimulates a deep integrating and healing process within the brain. This processing, which appears to take place at a reflexive or cellular level within the nervous system, brings about a de-conditioning of previously conditioned, maladaptive emotional and physiological responses. Brainspotting appears to stimulate, focus, and activate the body's inherent capacity to heal itself from trauma.

All of these methods can be directed at reducing distress but can also be utilized to establish and strengthen internal resources. For example, in EFT and BSFF, once negative affect and distress are reduced, positive affirmations can be installed. With BSP, clients can expand on existing positive resource states, or "pendulate" between resource states and trauma states to enable more gradual, graded processing and desensitization of intensely traumatic and emotionally charged issues and symptoms.

Mechanism of Action

Since Callahan's initial discovery, the mechanisms of EP have been further explored and defined. Feinstein (2018) explains that EP combines exposure therapy with interventions that reduce hyperarousal through acupressure and related techniques. This often leads to treatment outcomes that are faster and more powerful than techniques used in other exposure-based treatments such as relaxation or diaphragmatic breathing.

The underlying mechanism of action appears to be that tapping on those acupoints sends an electric signal to the amygdala, the emotional center of the brain that is associated with the fight-flight-freeze response and that also plays a role in memory storage. Research at Harvard Medical School on the mechanisms of acupressure found that rubbing, tapping, or applying pressure to specific acupoints sends deactivating signals to the amygdala, setting off a cascade of biochemical reactions that allow the nervous system to shift into a more relaxed state, essentially moving from sympathetic nervous system arousal to parasympathetic relaxation (Fang et al., 2009; Hui et al., 2000).

Additional research has demonstrated significant changes in the brain and body resulting from acupoint stimulation, including normalization of brain-wave patterns (Lambrou et al., 2003; Swingle, 2010); changes in heart rate variability, heart coherence, resting heart rate, and blood pressure (Bach et al., 2019); decreased cortisol levels (Church et al., 2012); shifts of blood flow in the brain (Stapleton, 2019); and changes in gene expression associated with improved health and mental health (Church et al., 2018; Maharaj, 2016).

An additional component of the tapping treatment that appears to benefit psychological issues, particularly trauma, is memory reconsolidation. According to Feinstein (2018), after the amygdala receives the deactivating signal from tapping, it in turn signals the hippocampus, the part of the brain responsible for memory storage, to re-record the memory of the event or issue without the emotional distress—a phenomenon known as memory consolidation. This causes the neural pathways that initiated the stress response to be permanently altered, allowing the person to encounter the trigger without limbic arousal, essentially extinguishing the stress response (Schiller et al., 2010).

In terms of the safety of tapping, Church (2013, p. 650) reported that a review of clinical trials with over 1,000 participants found that no "adverse events" had been reported. Therapists using EP in treating survivors of childhood sexual abuse have indicated that their clients preferred this approach because it lessened the chances of being flooded with traumatic material and becoming re-traumatized (Schulz, 2009; White, 2015).

Research on EP

Over 250 review articles, research studies, and meta-analyses have been published in professional, peer-reviewed journals on the topic of EP (ACEP, n.d.).

EP tapping modalities, such as EFT and TFT, have been shown in a number of studies to be effective for mitigating the effects of PTSD and trauma, depression, anxiety, addiction, and other conditions often seen in mental health and addiction treatment (Feinstein, 2018; Sakai et al., 2001). Research on EP and addiction indicates that EFT has a beneficial effect on reducing cravings and emotional triggers to addictive behavior, such as anxiety and depression (Church & Brooks, 2010; Church & Brooks, 2013; Stapleton et al., 2020).

Stapleton has published a series of studies on food cravings in overweight and obese adults, demonstrating that EFT can effectively reduce food cravings, with fMRI imaging illustrating decreased activity in the limbic region, the parts of the brain believed to be involved in addictive behavior (Stapleton et al., 2019).

Much of the research on addiction and EP has been on food cravings, but EFT has also been successfully used to help individuals quit smoking by addressing such client concerns as cravings, withdrawal symptoms, relapse triggers, fears, discomfort, and more (Stapleton et al., 2013). Feinstein (2021) outlines a protocol for applying EP with substance use disorders according to the recognized stages of change. Specific targets of the protocol include: (a) relieving cravings and reprogramming maladaptive emotional or behavioral responses to triggers; (b) addressing unresolved emotional issues that were precursors to substance abuse; (c) instilling skills for better managing pain, stress, anxiety, and cravings; and (d) increasing self-esteem and confidence.

Several meta-analyses of EP treatments have been conducted on anxiety, depression, and PTSD, respectively. Of 14 randomized controlled trials (RCTs) examining acupoint tapping in the treatment of anxiety disorders, a large combined pre- to posttreatment effect size of 1.23 was indicated (Clond, 2016). For depression treated with tapping, another large effect size of 1.85 was found in a meta-analysis of 12 RCTs (Nelms & Castel, 2016). For PTSD, a very large effect size of 2.96 was reported in seven RCTs (Sebastian & Nelms, 2016).

When EP was compared to other evidence-based treatments such as CBT across a variety of mental health issues, eight studies found that the EP outcomes were equivalent or superior to the CBT outcomes, with results sustained over time (Feinstein, 2018). Feinstein highlights that results in a number of studies were obtained more quickly with EP methods than with CBT, requiring fewer treatment sessions, which may indicate a cost-effectiveness benefit of these techniques.

In a comparison with EMDR, both approaches demonstrated large effect sizes in fewer than four sessions (Karatzias et al., 2011). This is of particular note, as the Brainspotting (BSP) technique used at Avery Lane derives from EMDR. It may be that the eye movement involved in EMDR and BSP functions similarly to the eye movements in the 9 Gamut sequence of EFT (D. Church, personal communication, January 29, 2021).

These emerging research findings suggest that EFT may be an effective and fast-acting adjunct to addiction treatment by reducing the severity of psychological distress, processing unresolved trauma, and reducing the cravings for substances.

Avery Lane Treatment Program

Avery Lane for Women is a private, eight-bed residential treatment facility in Novato, California, in the San Francisco Bay Area, offering 30 to 90-day residential treatment stays in addition to outpatient services for up to 12 women (averylanewomensrehab.com). Avery Lane serves women with co-occurring substance use and mental health disorders, particularly trauma. It offers four levels of care including detoxification, residential, partial hospitalization, and intensive outpatient treatment with the option of supportive housing in a sober living environment.

The program offers all the traditional gold-standard substance abuse treatments such as motivational interviewing (MI), MAT, CBT, dialectical behavioral therapy (DBT), relapse prevention, process groups, and 12-Step and other self-help groups, in addition to a variety of complementary alternative modalities including massage, Reiki, Access Bars, yoga, mindfulness, meditation, art therapy, nature therapy, and equine-assisted therapy. Trauma-specific curricula include *Seeking Safety* and *Beyond Trauma*, and clients also participate in classes such as Family Systems, Anger Management, Codependency, Medical Education, Life Skills, and Conscious Recovery.

Clients in residential treatment typically receive two individual therapy sessions per week, while outpatient clients receive one. Unlike other dual diagnosis programs, trauma processing is often started much earlier in treatment, in a safe, contained environment with 24/7 staff support. The program has also been designed to offer the unique possibility for the client to remain with the same therapist across all levels of care, which is not typically seen in other programs. This allows a strong therapeutic bond to form between client and therapist, and for the therapeutic work to deepen over a longer period of time. Many clients also choose to see their therapist in private practice after they complete treatment, another feature generally prohibited by other treatment centers.

Energy Psychology at Avery Lane

The EP techniques that this author (who is the clinical director at Avery Lane) has been using personally and in private practice since the year 2000 include EFT, TFT, BSFF, Tapas Acupressure Technique (TAT), Neuro Emotional Technique (NET), Reiki, Access Consciousness, and, though not officially recognized as an EP technique but seeming to function in a similar way, BSP. Several of these modalities have been brought into the treatment at Avery Lane. The EP modalities most frequently used are EFT, BSFF, and BSP.

When providing treatment to this population, third parties such as insurance companies and accrediting agencies generally require the use of evidence-based therapies. With its growing body of supportive clinical and research evidence, EP meets those criteria. According to ACEP (n.d.), methods such as EFT and TFT are both evidence-based and in the top 10% in terms of published research for psychotherapy modalities.

Applying the standards defined by the American Psychological Association's (APA) Division 12 Task Force on Empirically Validated Treatments, EFT has demonstrated efficacy for anxiety, depression, PTSD, and phobias (Feinstein, 2018). In 2016, TFT was validated by NREPP (the National Repository of Evidence Based Practices and Procedures, a division of SAMHSA) as an evidence-based treatment. EFT was under consideration with the same agency until the agency was defunded several years ago (ACEP, n.d.).

At Avery Lane, the EP tools are incorporated into group and individual therapy sessions. This author facilitates two EP groups per week, one for residential and one for outpatient clients. In the groups, clients learn the science behind tapping and how it works and engage in group tapping exercises on a variety of topics relevant to substance use and mental health treatment. They also process personal issues at the group level with facilitation by the group leader.

All clinical staff are taught the EP methods in designated training sessions, and they often sit in on EP groups to learn and support the use of the tools in other groups and individual sessions. All therapists are trained in BSP techniques as well.

All the primary coping skills (including the EP tools) the clients learn are also taught to the front-line staff, that is, the residential counselors (RCs), which is not usually done at other treatment centers. The RCs are then able to support the clients in using the tools whenever they are activated, for example, on outings, when clients are troubled with symptoms, and during interpersonal conflicts brought on by communal living situations. Staff in EP training get the same handouts the clients receive and are encouraged to use the tools themselves to deal with their own issues, especially in the treatment setting when clients trigger countertransference. Tapping therefore benefits not only clients but also clinicians and program staff; they can learn to tap on themselves to reduce stress and increase their sense of peace and well-being. They then get to model for the clients how to handle difficult situations with healthier coping strategies using role-plays.

EP in Psychotherapy for Co-Occurring Disorders

In terms of psychotherapy, the Avery Lane program espouses a holistic and comprehensive approach to treating the physical, mental, emotional, and spiritual components of any issue, including addiction, anxiety, depression, PTSD, and trauma. EP techniques are an integral part of this approach.

The EP tools may be readily used in conjunction with other standard treatments to address the Four C's of addiction: craving, compulsion, loss of control, and continued use despite consequences (Amen & Smith, 2010). They can also enhance the ability of motivational interviewing (Miller & Rollnick, 2013) to explore and shift clients' ambivalence about change, to explore and clear their limiting beliefs about being able to change, and to address their fears, doubts, and worries about what will happen and what people will think of them if they do change.

Other applications of BSP or the EP tools for addiction include using EFT or BSFF to help clients reduce cravings to drink and use drugs; to mitigate physical pain that triggers cravings; to diminish feelings of anxiety, sadness, shame, or resentments that are triggers to use; to reframe and clear limiting thoughts and beliefs, such as "I'm not enough" or "I'm a bad person," that underlie addictive behaviors; and to minimize feelings of emptiness or disconnection from self/others/Higher Power.

Therapists vary in their levels of expertise with the various techniques, and some favor certain approaches over others. Clients also tend to align with some tools more readily than others, and therapists respect their wishes. This author uses clinical intuition and client preference when choosing which technique to utilize in a given session.

EP can also be combined with other standardized treatments such as CBT. In the EP group, we do a CBT thought record then use EP techniques such as tapping or BSFF to further release any remaining emotional distress. The tools can also be used to treat psychological reversals, a concept originating from Callahan (1995), which addresses self-sabotage in the form of subconscious beliefs (e.g., secondary gains a client gets from keeping the problem, or concepts like "It's not safe for me to let this go," "I don't deserve to be free of this," or "I don't like who I'd be if I changed this."). EP can also be used to install positive cognitions such as affirmations.

In trauma-specific groups such as *Seeking Safety* or *Beyond Trauma*, when clients get triggered by the material being discussed, they can stop and tap to reduce their level of distress. Tapping is also used to help clients who are dissociated get grounded and back into their bodies.

Clinical application of these tools at Avery Lane has shown that when clients can reduce the emotional distress that triggers their substance use, they can effectively curtail their addictive behaviors, including releasing the idea that the alcohol or drug will make them feel better, reminding themselves they have other choices, and engaging in positive self-talk and affirmations. The tools are therefore taught to the clients to use as coping skills for emotional self-regulation.

The EP techniques are also utilized in therapy to treat the underlying roots of presenting issues, which are often unresolved trauma or upset from the past that keeps getting retriggered in the present. They can be considered a form of somatic therapy that allows the body to release rapidly and effectively the stuck energies from trauma. The tools also assist clients in getting out of the hyperarousal of the nervous system associated with PTSD and the fight-flight-freeze response.

The benefit of using these nervous system calming techniques is that they allow a person's reasoning capacities and higher-order processing to come back online quickly to make safer and wiser choices than the dangerous or self-harming behaviors that had been used when the client was under duress. Clients can't think straight when they are intensely triggered and in a state of fight-flight-freeze, which is why many strategies like CBT do not seem to be very effective in those moments.

Materials and Methods

Avery Lane has retained the services of Vista Research Group (www.vista-research-group.com) to implement a variety of computer-administered client self-report measures at intake, discharge, and weekly throughout treatment. The standardized instruments utilized include the Patient Health Questionnaire depression module (PHQ-9; Kroenke et al. 2001), Generalized Anxiety Disorder–7 scale (GAD-7; Spitzer et al., 2006), PTSD Checklist-6 (PCL-6; Lang et al., 2012), Columbia–Suicide Severity Rating Scale (C-SSRS; Posner et al., 2011), and Eating Disorder Diagnostic Scale (EDDS; Stice et al., 2000), along with a number of nonstandardized questionnaires, including one to assess frequency of cravings to drink or use. Clients are asked to complete voluntarily the measures to assess their progress during treatment.

Demographics and Intake Statistics

Table 1 details the demographics of the 147 clients for whom data were collected in the period of November 2, 2017 to February 9, 2021.

With regard to primary drug of choice, 64% of clients in the data group reported their preferred substance as alcohol, 8% methamphetamines, 7% opiates, 3% cannabis, 3% benzodiazepines, 3% heroin, 3% amphetamines, 2% cocaine, 1% inhalants, and 6% other.

Addiction level was identified as severe for 52% of clients (meeting every criteria established by the DSM-5), moderately severe (endorsing 6-10 DSM-5 criteria) for 40%, moderate for 3%, and mild for 3%, with only 1% of clients reporting no substance use disorder.

Thirty-nine percent of clients reported this was their first substance treatment episode, 9% had one prior treatment experience, 26% had two to three episodes, 18% between four and six episodes, 6% had seven to nine episodes, and 1% reported 10 or more prior treatment episodes.

Table 1. *Client Demographics*

Age	Age range: 18–73 Median age: 39
Ethnicity	86% Caucasian, non-Hispanic 3% Hispanic/Latina 3% Asian 1% African-American 8% Other
Marital status	42% Single/never married 33% Married 15% Divorced 8% Separated 1% Widowed
Highest education attained	1% Doctorate degree 7% Master's degree 35% Bachelor's degree 12% Associate's degree 26% Some college 9% High school/GED 1% Did not graduate high school 9% Other
Employment	25% Employed full-time 11% Employed part-time 9% Working in the home 4% Going to school 2% Working and going to school 26% Not working or going to school by choice 6% Not working or going to school due to being fired or kicked out 16% Other
Living situation	62% Stable, living in own home or dorm room 14% Stable, living in family's home 6% Stable, other 4% Stable, living in a sober living environment 8% Unstable, other 6% Unstable, moving from place to place 1% Homeless

Regarding mental health symptoms, at the time of intake, 88% of 140 clients reported depressive symptoms (40% rating their depression as severe, 27% moderately severe, 11% moderate, 10% mild), 93% cited anxiety symptoms (50% severe, 24% moderate, 19% mild), and 83% reported trauma symptoms (69% severe PTSD, 6% probable PTSD, 2% possible PTSD, 6% mild PTSD).

With regard to suicidality, 53% of clients reported that they wished they were dead or would go to sleep and not wake up; 35% admitted to suicidal thoughts; 24% had thought about how they would kill themselves; 14% intended to act on those thoughts; 10% started working out the details; 10% intended to carry out the plan; and 10% had recently prepared, started, or attempted suicide.

Eating disordered behaviors included 35% of clients reporting binge eating (distressful nighttime eating and eating large amounts of food and losing control) and 45% reporting compensatory behaviors (fasting, vomiting, intense exercise to counteract eating, laxative/diuretic use), with 4% reporting low body mass index/possible anorexia.

Overall, the population treated is a group of severely impaired, dually diagnosed women, the majority of whom have had previous courses of treatment, and who are dealing with a number of serious mental health and substance use disorders, especially depression, anxiety, trauma, suicidality, eating disordered behaviors, and PTSD.

Results

The median length of stay for all clients was 63 days ($n = 119$), 33 days for those in detox/residential levels of care ($n = 63$), and 101 days for those attending partial hospitalization/intensive outpatient levels of care ($n = 56$).

Seventy-seven percent of all clients successfully completed treatment ($n = 130$), 8% left early against medical advice, 8% were terminated for administrative reasons, 5% were transferred to another treatment program, and 2% were discharged for other reasons. When compared to other private treatment programs that employ the services of Vista Research Group ($n = 37{,}443$), Avery Lane achieved similar but slightly better outcomes; the data for the other programs included an average of 73% of clients who successfully completed treatment, 11% left early against medical advice, 5% were terminated for administrative reasons, 4% were transferred to another treatment program, and 5% were discharged for other reasons (M. O'Sullivan, personal communication, April 29, 2021).

When compared to national statistics, Avery Lane's outcomes are significantly better than norms provided in the 2017 Treatment Episode Data Set–Discharges (TEDS-D; SAMHSA, 2019), which cite a low 41% successful completion rate, with 30% dropping out of treatment, and 22% transferred to further treatment. Note that the TEDS data set consists primarily of publicly funded treatment programs receiving funding from the federal and/or state governments. Avery Lane is a private corporation that receives revenue from insurance and private pay.

Progress in treatment, as measured by comparing the self-report measures at intake and discharge (or last survey prior to discharge), indicate that a significant improvement in mental health symptoms occurred for the majority of clients ($n = 116$–123). Depression scores on the PHQ-9 dropped from an average of 79% at intake to 16% at last survey, $p < .001$ (Figure 1). Anxiety scores on the GAD-7 fell from 73% to 8%, $p < .001$ (Figure 2). PCL-6 scores for trauma symptoms went down from 76% to 30%, below the probable PTSD threshold, $p < .001$ (Figure 3). Suicidality levels measured by the C-SSRS fell from a high of 53% of clients at intake wishing they were

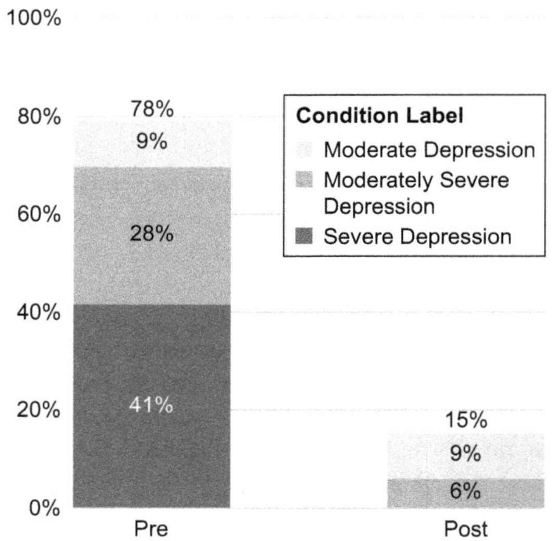

Figure 1. Patient progress on progression symptoms (PHQ-9), $n = 116$.

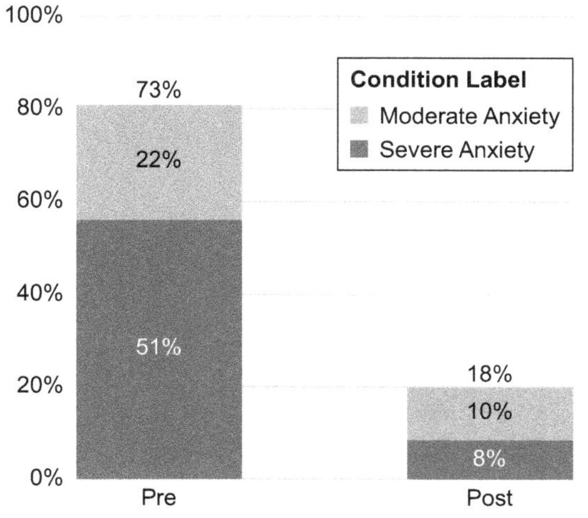

Figure 2. Patient progress on anxiety symptoms (GAD-7), $n = 116$.

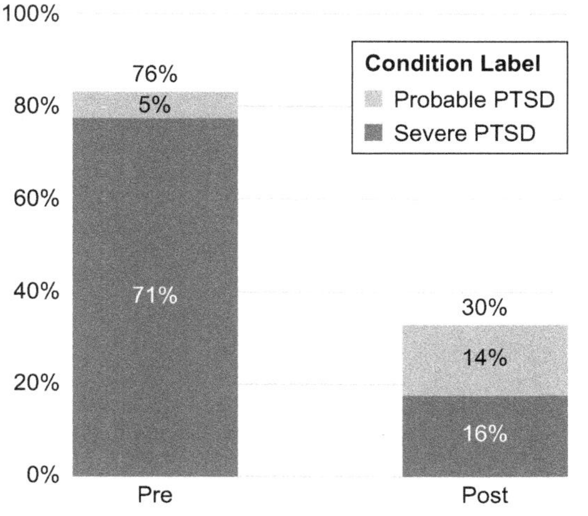

Figure 3. Patient progress on trauma symptoms (PCL-6), $n = 116$.

dead to 11% at last survey, $p < .001$, with similar reductions in other suicidal behaviors (Figure 4). For the EDDS, eating disordered behaviors showed binge eating rates dropping from 33% to 11%, $p = .01$, and compensatory behaviors with a drop from 41% to 11%, $p = .074$ (Figure 5).

Client Feedback

Overall, 82% of clients who came to Avery Lane reported being "very satisfied" with their treatment; 12% were "somewhat satisfied," 3% were "neutral," and 3% were "somewhat" or "very unsatisfied" (see Figure 6).

With regard to the use of EP methods, at first some clients were skeptical and judged the techniques to be strange. They reported, however, that it was highly beneficial to learn about the science behind EP approaches like EFT. Then when they tried it in groups or individual sessions and experienced stress relief in minutes (faster than a drink or pill), they were usually convinced. Clients were drinking and using primarily to quell

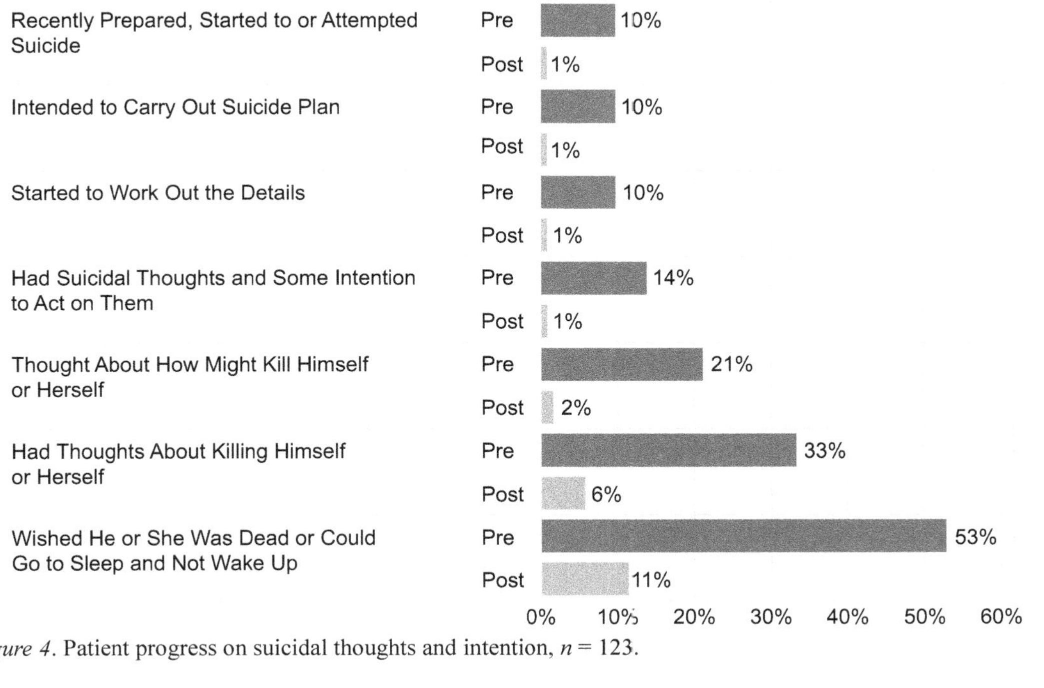

Figure 4. Patient progress on suicidal thoughts and intention, $n = 123$.

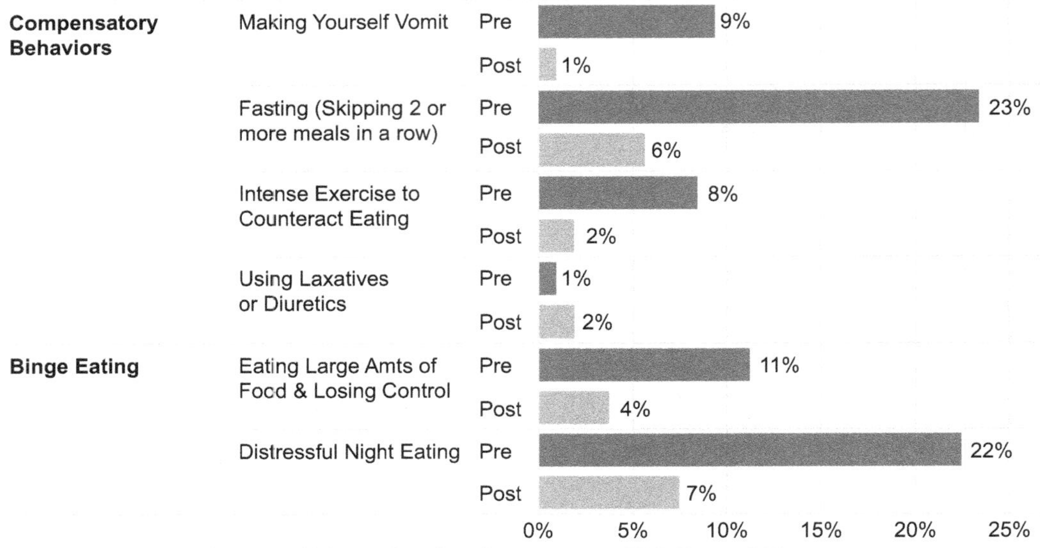

Figure 5. Percent of patients exhibiting eating disorder symptoms (EDDS), $n = 107$.

feelings of depression, anxiety, low self-esteem, shame, and anger, or to deal with symptoms of trauma and PTSD. When they discovered that they could use these tools to change the way they feel in a healthier way, they were empowered and their self-esteem and self-efficacy began to increase.

This strategy appears to be generating dramatic results. Clients are making significant changes in healing their traumas, limiting beliefs, and low self-esteem, and improving their relationships and interpersonal communication. Staff are grateful for the tools and feeling empowered to help the clients without going into compassion fatigue and codependency.

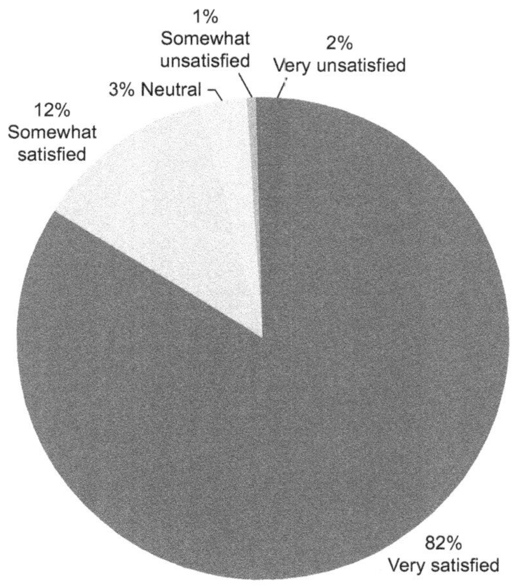

Figure 6. Patient satisfaction with treatment, $n = 518$.

Some specific quotes culled from client satisfaction surveys include:

"I feel like I'm learning a lot toward rewiring the way my brain thinks about myself and addiction and learning tools to deal with anxiety."

"Local, small, female-centered, alternative coping skill modalities, thorough exit plan—best care I have received in a treatment environment."

"Am learning sooo much. Also I love the variety of the treatment. Different teachers, different methods. This is good for me because I don't believe any one thing is going to help me, it's going to be a combination."

"I'm so grateful I got to come here…Clearing old unprocessed trauma energy is critical to my sobriety, and it's been done in a very organized manner here. Yay!"

"[My therapist] is amazing and the Brainspotting works wonders! I felt very comfortable and safe with her and she helped me through difficult traumas and memories that led me to use drugs until I came into recovery. She worked with me by being gentle and kind. I hope I can continue (and afford) to work with her after I leave Avery Lane because I admire her and the work she is doing with brain therapy. I find it fascinating even though I have to put the work into the sessions I always feel a level of self-empowerment and worthiness which I wasn't sure I was capable of feeling."

"The holistic approach with intensive trauma work has been incredibly effective...my therapist seems to intuitively understand. I've never felt so safe, loved, and understood in my life. I've found peace. Currently they are working on helping me maintain that sense of peace for longer stretches at a time... I have hope again."

Therapist Feedback

Here is what a few of the therapists at Avery Lane (who previously had little to no experience with EP tools) have said about using these techniques:

Therapist #1. "When first introduced to EP, I began using the tools on myself. I was amazed at how quickly I felt a positive shift in thoughts, sensations, and feelings. Each time I used the tools, I had the same positive results. It was as if a reset button had been pushed which allowed me to be more present and focused. I began offering the tools to my clients and each reported similar experiences and I noticed they continued to use the tools autonomously between sessions. The tools were especially effective in clients with trauma by decreasing stress, anxiety and increasing emotion regulation, giving clients a sense of empowerment and safety.

"Clients in treatment have experienced similar results and have the added benefit of learning and using these tools as a group and witnessing a reduction of symptoms in each other. Because these tools activate mind and body processes simultaneously, clients are better able to make use of their limited time in treatment for real change and healing."

Therapist #2. "The biggest notice with EP tools for clients and myself is the instant reduction in anxiety in the moment (short-term gain). Secondary long-term gain seems to be the increase in self-confidence and/or self-esteem that contributes to their belief they can stay sober because they have tools to self-regulate."

Therapist #3. "As for my experience as a therapist, I can say that EP enhances my ability to empower clients to directly experience, internalize, and regenerate the kinds of shifts that bring deep and lasting change. Beliefs, in my experience as a therapist, are not readily moved. Staying on the level of simple 'talk therapy' is relatively limiting when I can, conversely, incorporate energetic neurobiological regulation techniques to facilitate a client experiencing a more whole-being consciousness of what is possible. Then, with that felt experience, with that belief in the practicality of these tools, clients are able to continue developing on their own, as empowered and creative beings, rather than feeling quite so dependent on a therapist for scaffolding psychological flexibility. Anecdotally, I consistently see far greater/deeper evolution in my clients between sessions when they use EP tools, as compared to those who do not. No question."

Case Studies

Here are a couple of examples of specific clients treated with these EP techniques.

Client #1. This client is a 36-year-old female with mental health diagnoses of severe major depressive disorder, PTSD, and generalized anxiety disorder, with polysubstance use including opioid (IV heroin and Oxycontin), alcohol, and cannabis use disorders. Prior to treatment, she had not worked for over two years as a health care professional, was isolated in her home alone, malnourished, and not functioning. She reported a long history of physical and emotional abuse from family members throughout her life and cited symptoms of severe depression, passive suicidal ideation, low motivation, and feelings of hopelessness at intake, along with PTSD symptoms of flashbacks, hypervigilance, intrusive thoughts, exaggerated blame of self for causing the trauma, emotional distress, high levels of anxiety and psychomotor agitation, and difficulty experiencing positive affect.

Client #1 participated in our detox/residential program for 52 days, partial hospitalization program (PHP) for 40 days, and intensive outpatient program (IOP) for 45 days. In that time, she attended a total of 221 treatment groups, including 21 EP groups. She received 15 individual therapy sessions focused on treatment goals, case management, aftercare planning, family dynamics, and more, and 21 individual therapy sessions with this author utilizing techniques such as BSP and EFT. These sessions were focused on trauma processing (including her family abuse and the unexpected death of her Avery Lane therapist while in treatment), negative self-cognitions, high levels of shame and guilt, and extremely low self-esteem. The client also diligently practiced the EP and other tools she learned in treatment and applied them to her life on a daily basis.

This client made significant progress in treatment. At the time of her successful discharge from outpatient treatment, she was stable on MAT and had seven months sober, was able to quit smoking tobacco, built a sober support system, and learned to set healthier boundaries with abusive family members. She realized that her primary abuser was a malignant narcissist and she was able to release feelings of self-blame and shame that she had deserved the abuse.

With regard to her mental health, she reported a remission of depressive symptoms and suicidal ideation, and a significant reduction of anxiety and PTSD symptoms. She began to access positive emotions, engaging in pleasurable activities and experiencing spiritual reconnection and growth. She reported having a sense for the first time of seeing herself in old age; she had previously felt that she would commit suicide before then. Her motivation level increased and she took steps toward preparing to go back to work.

On her Vista self-report surveys, her depression scores fell from 16/27 (moderately severe depression) to 4/27 (no depression), anxiety decreased from 12/21 (moderate anxiety) to 2/21 (minimal anxiety), trauma symptoms reduced from 21/30 (severe) to 7/30 (low), suicidal thoughts fell from 3/7 to 0/7 (no suicidal thoughts), eating disordered behavior (restricting) dropped from four times a week to 0, and frequency and severity of cravings for drugs and alcohol decreased from moderate to mild.

Client #2. This client is a 33-year-old woman with PTSD, major depressive disorder, alcohol use disorder, and significant binge use history of opioids and cocaine. The client had previously completed 26 days of residential treatment at another program, maintained eight months of sobriety, and was enrolled in an IOP program when she relapsed. Triggered by grief over the recent death of a grandparent who had raised her, she relapsed on a binge of alcohol, opioids, and cocaine and was found passed out on a bathroom floor. She sought treatment due to awareness of need and willingness finally to address her unresolved trauma and grief.

This client reported an extensive history of trauma, especially in childhood. She grew up with addicted parents and was physically, emotionally, and sexually abused. She was removed from home at age 7 to live with her grandparents, and the family member who sexually abused her went to prison. Since that time, she experienced PTSD symptoms of intrusive memories and flashbacks, frequent nightmares, and hypervigilance, which led her to use substances to access a sense of relief from chronic and exhausting anxiety and shame. While she took on perfectionistic traits, including workaholism, to distract from worry and shame, she would feel compelled to become intoxicated when she was not otherwise occupied.

She reported that she felt such shame about her history of abuse that she struggled to connect with others, unable to allow herself to be vulnerable enough for others to get to know her or support her in an intimate way, leading to social isolation. She also exhibited poor boundaries, with codependent tendencies and a history of intimate partner violence as an adult.

After the death of her grandparent, the client's shame and emotional isolation increased and depression ensued, marked by anhedonia, reduced social activity, and severely restricted eating. She also exhibited symptoms of severe anxiety, unable to make eye contact or speak in groups when she first arrived to treatment.

The client participated in 32 days of detox/residential treatment, followed by 15 days of PHP sessions. She attended a total of 78 treatment groups, including eight EP groups. She received 11 individual therapy sessions, which included one BSP and two EFT tapping-focused sessions for grief and trauma processing.

She responded positively to the scientific explanation of EFT and began to use it to regulate her anxiety, which led her to experience empowerment over her automatic thoughts and core negative beliefs. She was able to use tapping to process through her guilt and move into a more empowered energy. Within one to two weeks, she also exhibited a remarkable shift in her willingness to share with vulnerability; she was able to speak openly about her abuse history and transformed her feelings of shame. She also used tapping to work through codependent and perfectionist tendencies getting in the way of creating and holding healthy boundaries. This resulted in an increase in self-care and self-respect, including building supportive relationships and a reduction in workaholic behavior.

With regard to her grief, Client #2 reported a shift to a perspective of gratitude for those she had lost and a renewed connection to them, even in her dreams. She also reported feeling a sense of hope that she could enjoy her life moving forward, which had been altogether absent for quite some time. She identified as having a spiritual awakening in treatment, and stated "Avery Lane has opened so many doors for me about recovery that I never knew about before."

Overall, the client experienced a remission in symptoms of depression and PTSD intrusion (nightmares, hypervigilance, and flashbacks) and, with her new tools, was able to cope with infrequent situational anxiety. Her reported isolative behavior improved and she increased healthy recreation and social interaction. At discharge, she reported feeling at peace with a knowing that she deserves to feel hope and joy, and does not need to accept suffering as she used to believe.

Client #2's excellent progress in a relatively short period of time is corroborated by her Vista survey results. Her self-reported depression scores fell from 23/27 (severe depression) to 0/27 (no depression), anxiety reduced from 12/21 (moderate anxiety) to 0/21 (none), symptoms of trauma went from 19/30 (severe) to 6/30 (minimal), eating disordered behavior (restricting) dropped from seven plus times per week to 0, and cravings for drugs and alcohol stayed consistent at almost none.

Conclusion

In working for over 20 years in the addiction treatment field, both as a clinician and as an administrator, this author has witnessed time and again that the majority of clients who present for substance abuse treatment suffer with co-occurring disorders, an observation that is backed by research (NIDA, 2020). They typically lack coping skills to manage effectively their negative thoughts and emotions, which are the primary triggers for their substance use. If their mental health symptoms are not addressed and well managed, clients will rarely be able to sustain long-term abstinence.

Furthermore, unresolved trauma is present in the vast majority of clinical cases. Symptoms such as hypervigilance come from an overactive nervous system that leaves clients in a constant state of fight-flight-freeze. This is a primary reason why many clients are self-medicating with drugs and alcohol. If they don't learn how to rewire and re-regulate that trauma response, they won't stay sober. Research cited in this paper supports these observations.

Research and clinical practice suggest there is a need for effective, holistic, comprehensive approaches that address the physical, mental, emotional, and spiritual components of these conditions. EP offers that, providing clients with empowering tools for emotional self-regulation and deeper trauma processing on all levels. EP techniques are often exceedingly rapid, have little to no adverse effects, and are usually experienced as self-empowering by therapists and clients alike.

Some of the benefits of EP reported in the literature and corroborated by the work at Avery Lane include: (a) a reduction and elimination of the effects of trauma more quickly and effectively than traditional talk therapy and other evidence-based approaches, (b) increased access to insight and positive cognitions that were obscured by trauma, and (c) an increase in a sense of self-control and confidence in knowing they can regulate their emotions on their own without the aid of drugs and alcohol (Feinstein, 2018).

The population at Avery Lane is a group of severely impaired, dually diagnosed women, the majority of whom have had previous courses of treatment, and who are dealing with a number of serious mental health and substance use disorders, especially depression, anxiety, trauma, suicidality, eating disordered behaviors, and PTSD. While at first some clients may have been skeptical about EP, once they learned about the science and research supporting it and they tried it for themselves, they became more open to applying the tools to a variety of areas, including cravings, mental health symptoms, core limiting beliefs, and motivation to change. When they discovered that they could use these coping tools to change the way they feel in a healthier way, they were empowered and their self-esteem and self-efficacy began to increase, leading to improved relationships, interpersonal communication, and overall quality of life.

Specific results obtained at Avery Lane for this study include statistically significant reductions in self-reported levels of depression, anxiety, PTSD, and suicidality, with $p < .001$ for most measures (except the eating disordered behaviors), particularly compensatory behaviors. The results for eating disorders (ED) may be because they are not generally a focus of treatment at Avery Lane, staff are not specialists in this area, and clients with more severe ED behaviors are typically referred out to ED specialty programs.

The Avery Lane data support results from other studies on addictive behaviors including food cravings (Stapleton et al., 2019) and smoking cessation (Stapleton et al., 2013). Given that persons with addictive behaviors are often attempting to "self-medicate" emotional distress and mental health symptoms with substances, our results further corroborate the work of Church and Brooks (2010, 2013) and Stapleton et al. (2020), which suggest that reducing the intensity of anxiety, depression, and PTSD symptomology has a beneficial effect on reduction in substance use. Similar to the Reset program at Fort Hood (Libretto et al., 2015), it appears that Avery Lane's integrated approach to PTSD treatment, which includes traditional psychotherapeutic techniques, EP, and CAM, is highly effective in reducing symptoms of depression, anxiety, PTSD, and more.

Limitations of this study include a relatively small and less demographically diverse sample group (n = 123), lack of control or other comparison groups, and an inability to differentiate which techniques may have been most effective in achieving the strong results obtained. Longer follow-up to see if results are maintained over time would have also been useful, and to this end, Avery Lane has recently employed Vista Research Group to begin collecting these data.

As science continues to learn more about how the brain functions through brain imaging and the study of epigenetics, the mechanisms underlying EP techniques and how these techniques can positively affect the brains of dually diagnosed individuals who have been struggling with addiction and mental health disorders will become clearer. Further studies are needed to validate EP techniques for this population and to assess their potential as a viable cost-effective approach that can shorten the length of treatment.

Recommended treatment guidelines for facilities wishing to add EP to their current treatment approach include the following: Hire one or more therapists who are already well versed and skilled in EP. Have those clinicians demonstrate the techniques to other staff (including frontline staff), use client role-plays, and have staff practice on one another with their own personal issues and issues of transference/countertransference that arise when working with clients. If the EP tools are taught in therapy groups, have other staff attend as well so they can observe how the experienced practitioner teaches the skills and utilizes them with specific client issues. Supplement group and individual sessions with YouTube videos and other resources such as videos, audios, and handouts from the annual Tapping World Summit (thetappingsolution.com), ACEP's Resources for Resilience (www.r4r.support), and EFT Universe (eftuniverse.com), among others. Be sure the trained EP practitioner is available for case consultation on an ongoing basis and that refreshers or additional trainings are offered periodically to grow and reinforce skills.

This author has found that staff buy-in is very important, especially when trying to introduce clients to these nontraditional treatment methods. It may take some time to convince clinicians and counselors (especially those entrenched in their own preferred approaches) that these sometimes strange-appearing techniques are effective. Explaining the research and science behind EP can be very beneficial in this regard. Inviting staff to experiment with the tools for their own issues and observing the positive results the clients get with them is key to shifting their perspective. As a majority of staff become open and supportive of the tools, others will often get on board as well. At Avery Lane, staff have expressed gratitude for the EP tools and feel more empowered to help the clients without going into compassion fatigue, vicarious traumatization, and codependency. This has ultimately improved staff morale and employee retention.

In the four years since its inception, Avery Lane has successfully integrated EP as standard of practice in our treatment program, and it is our hope that other programs will be inspired by our experience to try these approaches for themselves. As one therapist's thesis on EP for treating trauma stated: "Energy psychology has the potential to catalyze a process of transformation that results in a lived experience of serenity and flourishing" (White, 2015, p. 2). Many of our clients and staff have experienced these powerful results thanks to EP.

The data and clinical results from Avery Lane are consistent with those derived from meta-analyses, clinical trials, and experiences at other treatment centers. This body of literature demonstrates that EP is a powerful, evidence-based approach that sets the standard for effective addiction treatment.

References

Amen, D. G., & Smith, D. E. (2010). *Unchain your brain.* Irvine, CA: MindWorks Press.

Anglin, M. D., Hser, Y. I., & Grella, C. E. (1997). Drug addiction and treatment careers among clients in the Drug Abuse Treatment Outcome Study (DATOS). *Psychology of Addictive Behaviors, 11*(4), 308. doi:10.1037/0893-164X.11.4.308

Association of Comprehensive Energy Psychology (ACEP). (n.d.). Retrieved from www.energypsych.org

Bach, D., Groesbeck, G., Stapleton, P., Banton, S., Blickheuser, K., & Church, D. (2019). Clinical EFT (Emotional Freedom Techniques) improves multiple physiological markers of health. *Journal of Evidence-Based Integrative Medicine, 24.* doi:10.1177/2515690X18823691

Berenz, E. C., & Coffey, S. F. (2012). Treatment of co-occurring posttraumatic stress disorder and substance use disorders. *Current Psychiatry Reports, 14*(5), 469–477. doi:10.1007/s11920-012-0300-0

Boden, M. T., Kimerling, R., Kulkarni, M., Bonn-Miller, M. O., Weaver, C., & Trafton J. (2014). Coping among military veterans with PTSD in substance use disorder treatment. *Journal of Substance Abuse Treatment, 47*(2), 160–167. doi:10.1016/j.jsat.2014.03.006

Callahan, R. J. (1985). *Five minute phobia cure: Dr. Callahan's treatment for fears, phobias, and self-sabotage.* Blair, NE: Enterprise.

Callahan, R. J. (1995). A Thought Field Therapy (TFT) algorithm for trauma. *Traumatology, 1*(1), 7–13. doi:10.1177/153476569500100102

Church, D. (2013). Clinical EFT as an evidence-based practice for the treatment of psychological and physiological conditions. *Psychology, 4*(8), 645–654. doi:10.4236/psych.2013.48092

Church, D., & Brooks, A. J. (2010). The effect of a brief EFT (Emotional Freedom Techniques) self-intervention on anxiety, depression, pain and cravings in healthcare workers. *Integrative Medicine: A Clinician's Journal, 9*(5), 40–44.

Church, D., & Brooks, A. J. (2013). The effect of EFT (Emotional Freedom Techniques) on psychological symptoms in addiction treatment: A pilot study. *Journal of Scientific Research and Reports, 2*(1), 315–323. doi:10.9734/JSRR/2013/3500

Church, D., Yount, G., & Brooks, A. J. (2012). The effect of Emotional Freedom Techniques on stress biochemistry: A randomized controlled trial. *Journal of Nervous and Mental Disease, 200*(10), 891–896. doi:10.1097/NMD.0b013e31826b9fc1

Church, D., Yount, G., Rachlin, K., Fox, L., & Nelms, J. (2016). Epigenetic effects of PTSD remediation in veterans using clinical Emotional Freedom Techniques: A randomized controlled pilot study. *American Journal of Health Promotion, 32*(1), 112–122. doi:10.1177/0890117116661154

Clond, M. (2016). Emotional Freedom Techniques for anxiety: A systematic review with meta-analysis. *Journal of Nervous and Mental Disease, 204*(5), 388–395. doi:10.1097/NMD.0000000000000483

Cottler, L. B., Compton, W. M., Mager, D., Spitznagel, E. L., & Janca, A. (1992). Posttraumatic stress disorder among substance users from the general population. *American Journal of Psychiatry, 149*(5), 664–670. doi:10.1176/ajp.149.5.664

Craig, G., & Fowlie, A. (1995). *Emotional freedom techniques: The manual.* Sea Ranch, CA: Gary Craig.

Dawson, D. A. (1996). Correlates of past-year status among treated and untreated persons with former alcohol dependence: United States. *Alcoholism: Clinical and Experimental Research 20*(4), 771–779. doi:10.1111/j.1530-0277.1996.tb01685.x

DeMarce, J. M., Lash, S. J., Stephens, R. S., Grambow, S. C., & Burden, J. L. (2008). Promoting continuing care adherence among substance abusers with co-occurring psychiatric disorders following residential treatment. *Addictive Behaviors, 33*(9), 1104–1112. doi:10.1016/j.addbeh.2008.02.008

De Soto, C. B., O'Donnell, W. E., & De Soto, J. L. (1989). Long-term recovery in alcoholics. *Alcoholism: Clinical and Experimental Research, 13*(5), 693–697. doi:10.1111/j.1530-0277.1989.tb00406.x

Fang, J., Jin, Z., Wang, Y., Li, K., Kong, J., Nixon, E. E., … Hui, K. K.-S. (2009). The salient characteristics of the central effects of acupuncture needling: Limbic-paralimbic-neocortical network modulation. *Human Brain Mapping, 30*(4), 1196–1206. doi:10.1002/hbm.20583

Feinstein, D. (2018). Energy psychology: Efficacy, speed, mechanisms. *Explore: The Journal of Science and Healing, 15*(5), 340–351. doi:10.1016/j.explore.2018.11.003

Feinstein, D. (2021). Energy Psychology in the treatment of substance use disorders. In Rita Carroll (Ed.), *Complementary and integrative approaches to substance use disorders.* Hauppauge, NY: Nova Science.

Finney, J. W., & Moos, R. H. (1991). The long-term course of treated alcoholism: I. Mortality, relapse and remission rates and comparisons with community controls. *Journal of Studies on Alcohol, 52*(1), 44–54. doi:10.15288/jsa.1991.52.44

Grand, D. (2013). *Brainspotting: The revolutionary new therapy for rapid and effective change.* Boulder, CO: Sounds True.

Han, B., Compton, W. M., Blanco, C., & Colpe, L. J. (2017). Prevalence, treatment, and unmet treatment needs of US adults with mental health and substance use disorders. *Health Affairs, 36*(10), 1739–1747. doi:10.1377/hlthaff.2017.0584

Hser, Y. I., Anglin, M. D., Grella, C., Longshore, D., & Prendergast, M. L. (1997). Drug treatment careers. A conceptual framework and existing research findings. *Journal of Substance Abuse Treatment, 6,* 543–558. doi:10.1016/S0740-5472(97)00016-0

Hui, K. K., Liu, J., Makris, N., Gollub, R. L., Chen, A. J., Moore, C. I., … Kwong, K. K. (2000). Acupuncture modulates the limbic system and subcortical gray structures of the human brain: evidence from fMRI studies in normal subjects. *Human Brain Mapping, 9*(1), 13–25. doi:10.1002/(sici)1097-0193(2000)9:1<13::aid-hbm2>3.0.co;2-f

Karatzias, T., Power, K., Brown, K., McGoldrick, T., Begum, M., Young, J., … Adams, S. (2011). A controlled comparison of the effectiveness and efficiency of two psychological therapies for posttraumatic stress disorder: Eye Movement Desensitization and Reprocessing vs. Emotional Freedom Techniques. *Journal of Nervous and Mental Disease, 199*(6), 372–378. doi:10.1097/NMD.0b013e31821cd262

Kelly, T. M., & Daley, D. C. (2013). Integrated treatment of substance use and psychiatric disorders. *Social Work Public Health, 28,* 388–406. doi:10.1080/19371918.2013.774673

Kroenke, K., Spitzer, R. L., & Williams, J. B. (2001). The PHQ-9: Validity of a brief depression severity measure.

Journal of General Internal Medicine, 16(9), 606–613. doi:10.1046/j.1525-1497.2001.016009606.x

Lambrou, P. T., Pratt, G. J., & Chevalier, G. (2003). Physiological and psychological effects of a mind/body therapy on claustrophobia. *Subtle Energies and Energy Medicine, 14*(3), 239–251.

Lang, A. J., Wilkins, K., Roy-Byrne, P. P., Golinelli, D., Chavira, D., Sherbourne, C., … Stein, M. B. (2012). Abbreviated PTSD Checklist (PCL) as a guide to clinical response. *General Hospital Psychiatry, 34*(4), 332–338. doi:10.1016/j.genhosppsych.2012.02.003

Libretto, S., Hilton, L., Gordon, S., Zhang, W., & Wesch, J. (2015). Effects of integrative PTSD treatment in a military health setting. *Energy Psychology: Theory, Research, and Treatment, 7*(2), 33–44. doi:10.9769/EPJ.2015.11.1.SL

Maharaj, M. E. (2016). Differential gene expression after Emotional Freedom Techniques (EFT) treatment: A novel pilot protocol for salivary mRNA assessment. *Energy Psychology: Theory, Research, and Treatment, 8*(1), 17–32. doi:10.9769/EPJ.2016.8.1.MM

McGovern, M. P., Lambert-Harris, C., Gotham, H. J., Claus, R. E., & Xie, H. (2014). Dual diagnosis capability in mental health and addiction treatment services: An assessment of programs across multiple state systems. *Administration and Policy in Mental Health, 41*(2), 205–214. doi:10.1007/s10488-012-0449-1

Miller, W. R., & Rollnick, S. (2013). *Motivational interviewing: Helping people change.* New York, NY: Guilford Press.

Monahan, S., & Finney, J. (1996). Explaining abstinence rates following treatment for alcohol abuse. A quantitative synthesis of patient, research design, and treatment effects. *Addiction, 91,* 787–805. doi:10.1046/j.1360-0443.1996.9167876.x

Najavits, L. M., Weiss, R. D., & Shaw, S. R. (1997). The link between substance abuse and posttraumatic stress disorder in women: A research review. *American Journal on Addictions, 6*(4), 273–283. doi:10.1111/j.1521-0391.1997.tb00408.x

National Institute on Drug Abuse (NIDA). (2020). *Common comorbidities with substance use disorders research report.* Retrieved from https://www.drugabuse.gov/publications/research-reports/common-comorbidities-substance-use-disorders/introduction

Nelms, J., & Castel, D. (2016). A systematic review and meta-analysis of randomized and non-randomized trials of Emotional Freedom Techniques (EFT) for the treatment of depression. *Explore: The Journal of Science and Healing, 12*(6), 416–426. doi:10.1016/j.explore.2016.08.001

Nims, L. P., & Sotkin, J. (2003). *Be Set Free Fast!: A revolutionary new way to eliminate discomforts.* Santa Fe, NM: Sotkin Enterprises.

Posner, K., Brown, G. K., Stanley, B., Brent, D. A., Yershova, K. V., Oquendo, M. A., … Mann, J. J. (2011). The Columbia-Suicide Severity Rating Scale: Initial validity and internal consistency findings from three multisite studies with adolescents and adults. *American Journal of Psychiatry, 168*(12), 1266–1277. doi:10.1176/appi.ajp.2011.10111704

Sakai, C., Paperny, D., Mathews, M., Tanida, G., Boyd, G., Simons, A., … Nutter, L. (2001). Thought Field Therapy clinical applications: Utilization in an HMO in behavioral medicine and behavioral health services. *Journal of Clinical Psychology, 57*(10), 1229–1235. doi:10.1002/jclp.1088

Santucci, K. (2012). Psychiatric disease and drug abuse. *Current Opinion in Pediatrics, 24*(2), 233–237. doi:10.1097/MOP.0b013e3283504fbf

Schiller, D., Monfils, M. H., Raio, C. M., Johnson, D. C., Ledoux, J. E., & Phelps, E. A. (2010). Preventing the return of fear in humans using reconsolidation update mechanisms. *Nature, 463*(7277), 49–53. doi:10.1038/nature08637

Schulz, P. (2009). Integrating energy psychology into treatment for adult survivors of childhood sexual abuse. *Energy Psychology: Theory, Research, and Treatment, 1*(1), 15–22. doi:10.9769.EPJ.2009.1.1.KS

Sebastian, B., & Nelms, J. (2016). The effectiveness of Emotional Freedom Techniques in the treatment of posttraumatic stress disorder: A meta-analysis. *Explore: The Journal of Science and Healing, 13*(1), 16–25. doi:10.1016/j.explore.2016.10.001

Shapiro, F. (1995). *Eye Movement Desensitization and Reprocessing: Basic principles, protocols, and procedures* (1st ed.). New York, NY: Guilford Press.

Spitzer, R. L., Kroenke, K., Williams, J. B. W., & Löwe, B. (2006). A brief measure for assessing generalized anxiety disorder: The GAD-7. *Archives of Internal Medicine, 166*(10), 1092–1097. doi:10.1001/archinte.166.10.1092

Stapleton, P. (2019). *The science behind tapping: A proven stress management technique for the mind and body.* Carlsbad, CA: Hay House.

Stapleton, P., Buchan, C., Mitchell, I., McGrath, Y., Gorton, P., & Carter, B. (2019). An initial investigation of neural changes in overweight adults with food cravings after Emotional Freedom Techniques. *OBM Integrative and Complementary Medicine, 4*(1), 14.

Stapleton, P., Lilley-Hale, E., Mackintosh, G., & Sparenburg, E. (2020). Online delivery of Emotional Freedom Techniques for food cravings and weight management: 2-year follow-up. *Journal of Alternative and Complementary Medicine, 26*(2), 98–106. doi:10.1089/acm.2019.0309

Stapleton, P. B., Porter, B., & Sheldon, T. (2013). Quitting smoking: How to use Emotional Freedom Techniques. *International Journal of Healing and Caring, 13*(1), 1–16. Retrieved from http://www.ijhc.org/2016/01/quitting-smoking-how-touse-emotional-freedom-techniques-peta-stapleton-brett-porter-terri-sheldon/

Steenkamp, M. M., Litz, B. T., Hoge, C. W., Marmar, C. R. (2015). Psychotherapy for military-related PTSD: A review of randomized clinical trials. *JAMA, 314*(5), 489–500. doi:10.1001/jama.2015.8370

Stice, E., Telch, C. F., & Rizvi, S. L. (2000). Development and validation of the Eating Disorder Diagnostic Scale: A brief self-report measure of anorexia, bulimia, and binge-eating disorder. *Psychological Assessment, 12*(2), 123–131. doi:10.1037//1040-3590.12.2.123

Substance Abuse and Mental Health Services Administration (SAMHSA). (2019). *Treatment Episode Data Set (TEDS): 2017. Admissions to and Discharges from Publicly-Funded Substance Use Treatment.* Rockville, MD: Center for Behavioral Health Statistics and Quality, Substance Abuse and Mental Health Services Administration. Retrieved from https://wwwdasis.samhsa.gov/dasis2/teds_pubs/TEDS-2017-R.pdf

Substance Abuse and Mental Health Services Administration (SAMHSA). (2020). *Key substance use and mental health indicators in the United States: Results from the 2019 National Survey on Drug Use and Health* (HHS Publication No. PEP20-07-01-001). Rockville, MD: Center for Behavioral Health Statistics and Quality, Substance Abuse and Mental Health Services Administration. Retrieved from https://www.samhsa.gov/data/sites/default/files/reports/rpt29393/2019NSDUHFFRPDFWHTML/2019NSDUHFFR1PDFW090120.pdf

Swingle, P. (2010). EFT in the neurotherapeutic treatment of seizure disorders. *Energy Psychology: Theory, Research, and Treatment, 2*(1), 27–38. doi:10.9769.EPJ.2010.2.1.PGS

Torrens, M., Rossi, P. C., Martinez-Riera, R., Martinez-Sanvisens, D., & Bulbena, A. (2012). Psychiatric comorbidity and substance use disorders: Treatment in parallel systems or in one integrated system? *Substance Use and Misuse, 47*(8–9), 1005–1014. doi:10.3109/10826084.2012.663296

Vaillant, G. E. (1996). *The natural history of alcoholism revisited.* Cambridge, MA: Harvard University Press.

White, I. C. (2015). *It helps me to love my work: An interpretative phenomenological analysis of the senior therapist experience of using Energy Psychology in Psychotherapy for Trauma* (Master's thesis). Retrieved from http://hdl.handle.net/10788/2054

Wolpe, J. (1968). Psychotherapy by reciprocal inhibition. *Conditional Reflex: A Pavlovian Journal of Research and Therapy, 3*(4), 234–240.

REVIEW ARTICLE

Perceptions, Reflections, and Guidelines for Using Energy Psychology: A Distillation of 800+ Surveys and Interviews with Practitioners and Clients

David Feinstein, Ashland, Oregon, USA

Abstract
Energy Psychology is a modality for facilitating personal development that is increasingly being used in clinical settings as well as on a self-help basis. Credible estimates suggest that the number of therapists who are incorporating at least some Energy Psychology methods into their practices has grown into the tens of thousands, encompassing a wide range of theoretical orientations. More than 800 psychotherapists, counselors, or life coaches who use Energy Psychology have participated in online surveys or systematic interviews in 15 separate studies focusing on various aspects of the practice. From these investigations, as well as from client reports, the current study identifies and explores the following themes: speed, breadth, safety, therapeutic alliance, enhanced intuitive access, and spiritual attunement. In addition, nine implications for clinical practice were derived and are discussed under the topics of Treatment Focus, Use of Language, Resonance, Time Orientation, Cautions, Resistance to Tapping, Countertransference, Self-Help Applications, and Integrating Energy Psychology with Other Techniques.

Keywords: acupressure, anxiety, depression, Emotional Freedom Techniques, Energy Psychology, PTSD, stress, Thought Field Therapy, trauma

David Feinstein, PhD, is a clinical psychologist who has received nine national awards for his books on consciousness and healing, including the U.S. Book News Best Psychology/Mental Health Book of 2007. **Correspondence:** David Feinstein, PhD, 777 East Main Street, Ashland, OR 97520; df777@earthlink.net. **Disclosure:** The author conducts trainings, provides clinical services, and has written books related to the approach examined in this paper. **Acknowledgments:** The author wishes to thank John Freedom for his invaluable suggestions on an earlier draft of this paper.

Energy Psychology is a comprehensive system for emotional healing and psychological development that combines acupressure and other somatic techniques derived from ancient healing systems with contemporary psychotherapeutic methods (Gallo, 2004). Introduced in the 1980s, its most popular and well-researched formats include Emotional Freedom Techniques (EFT) and Thought Field Therapy (TFT), both of which teach clients how to stimulate acupuncture points (acupoints) by tapping on them. Use of these methods continues to expand, with a credible estimate suggesting that "tens of thousands" of therapists representing a wide range of theoretical orientations have incorporated at least some form of Energy Psychology into their practices (Leskowitz, 2016, p. 181).

As the approach has evolved, it can increasingly be understood within a scientifically informed clinical and neurological framework (Stapleton, 2019). A recent review of evidence found 113 of 115 peer-reviewed clinical trials to show statistically significant positive outcomes on standardized measures (Feinstein, 2021). The review also found strong effect sizes in meta-analyses of studies investigating the treatment of anxiety, depression, and posttraumatic stress disorder (PTSD), respectively; clinically favorable changes in cortisol levels, gene expression, and brain-wave patterns after a single session; and explanations of mechanisms of action that correspond with contemporary neurological understanding of psychological change. Nonetheless, the notion that tapping on the skin can impact serious psychological symptoms seems counterintuitive to many, consensus has not been reached on the biological mechanisms that would explain the positive outcomes being reported, and applications within conventional mental health treatment settings remain limited.

A way to understand a modality such as Energy Psychology is through the lived experiences of those who use it, either for themselves or as an instrument for helping others. This paper presents a review and analysis of the firsthand reports of more than 800 practitioners and clients. It examines six broad themes that were identified. It then discusses nine implications for clinical practice that were derived from the data.

The Data

Fifteen studies have used surveys or interviews to document and systematize the observations of hundreds of Energy Psychology practitioners. Ten were published in peer-reviewed journals, three were presented in master's theses or doctoral dissertations, and two are posted on websites. All 15 studies are listed below in two tables and cited in the references section. Seven of the studies used online surveys that received 1,058 responses from Energy Psychology therapists, counselors, or life coaches (Table 1), representing (based on an informed guess) at least 800 practitioners, since some may have participated in more than one survey. Another 79 individuals who use Energy Psychology provided in-depth interviews for an additional eight reports (Table 2). Of the estimated 800+ practitioners for whom these data exist, two frequent observations were that, as they began to use Energy Psychology, they were (a) surprised by how quickly the method seemed to work, and (b) they felt their effectiveness as clinicians was enhanced by the way complex problems could be separated into parts that are then efficiently addressed at their emotional core, one at a time, utilizing acupoint tapping.

Themes in the Practitioner Surveys and Interviews

Of course, the opinions and reflections of practitioners do not constitute scientific evidence. Bias, self-justification, and selective perceptions are inevitable. On the other hand, practitioners have an intimate vantage point about a method

Table 1. *Online Surveys of Energy Psychology Practitioners*

First Author	Date	Responders	Source
ACEP	2012	115 ACEP Members	Website
Church	2017	448 EFT Practitioners	Peer-Reviewed Journal
Feinstein	2005	18 Practitioners Identified as Leaders in the EP Field	Website
Feinstein	2016	294 ACEP Members	Peer-Reviewed Journal
Gaudiano	2012	149 Licensed Psychotherapists on Psychotherapy Listserves	Peer-Reviewed Journal
Schulz	2009	12 EP Practitioners Working/Childhood Sexual Abuse	Peer-Reviewed Journal
Stapleton	2017	22 Experienced EFT Practitioners	Peer-Reviewed Journal

Note: Totals: 1058 respondents in 7 survey studies. ACEP = Association for Comprehensive Energy Psychology; EFT = Emotional Freedom Techniques; EP = Energy Psychology.

Table 2. *Interviews with Energy Psychology Practitioners or Clients*

First Author	Date	Responders	Source
Chalmers	2015	12 Experienced EFT Practitioners	Masters Thesis
Hartung	2019	15 EFT Practitioners Working in Correctional Facilities	Peer-Reviewed Journal
Kalla	2018	8 EFT Practitioners Working with Chronic Disease Clients	Peer-Reviewed Journal
Kalla	2020	8 EFT Clients Presenting with Chronic Disease	Peer-Reviewed Journal
Mason	2012	5 Experienced Therapists Who Began Integrating EP	Peer-Reviewed Journal
Mitchell	2020	12 Experienced EFT Practitioners	Peer-Reviewed Journal
Nairn	2020	16 Experienced Therapists Who Began Integrating EFT	Doctoral Dissertation
White	2015	3 Experienced Therapists Who Began Integrating EP	Masters Thesis

Note: Totals: 79 participants in 8 interview studies. EFT = Emotional Freedom Techniques; EP = Energy Psychology.

that often goes deeper than and outpaces research findings. Six broad themes were identified: speed, breadth, safety, therapeutic alliance, enhanced intuitive access, and spiritual attunement. We will examine each individually before considering nine implications for clinical practice that can be derived from the surveys and interviews.

Speed

Participants in the interviews and surveys consistently expressed recognition and often surprise by the speed with which change can occur. Of 294 members of the Association for Comprehensive Energy Psychology (ACEP) responding to an online survey, three-fourths estimated that eliminating an unwanted physiological or emotional response to a specific trigger (i.e., a conditioned response such as in a phobia) typically requires less than an hour (Feinstein, 2016). Almost all said it could be accomplished within two or three sessions. When the trigger was associated with a traumatic event, 75% reported that, in their experience, the unwanted response could be eliminated within three sessions. Of 14 clinical trials using Energy Psychology in treating posttraumatic stress disorder (PTSD), half of the studies found statistically significant improvements after a single session (Sebastian & Nelms, 2017).

Twelve licensed psychologists, each in private practice for more than a decade, completed a detailed online survey on their use of Energy Psychology with adult survivors of childhood sexual abuse (Schulz, 2009). Each had been practicing for at least five years before taking training in Energy Psychology, and they were all already working with clients who had been sexually abused. All 12 reported that, of the many modalities available to them, they found anxiety-related symptoms "to be most effectively treated by energy psychology techniques" (p. 20). Although they might use other methods to help teach assertiveness or coping skills, working with acupoints was their most powerful and rapid tool for helping regulate the autonomic nervous system. Following Energy Psychology interventions, their clients experienced reductions in fear, stress, and anxiety; fewer flashbacks; improved sleep; and they were able to recall their traumatic experiences without being re-triggered.

While overcoming anxiety-related symptoms was the most frequently mentioned issue, a spectrum of distressful emotions was identified as responding with unusual speed to acupoint protocols, including guilt, shame, grief, jealousy, rejection, and feelings of isolation. One of the practitioners described EFT as being particularly "*transformational* in facilitating changes with men who have difficulties with anger" (Mason, 2012, p. 227). Anger is prevalent in correctional facilities, and a field study investigated the use of Energy Psychology with convicts in three settings (Hartung & Morales, 2019). It describes, for example, a parolee who was living in a halfway house and receiving treatment in a group with other offenders who also had violent histories. In one incident, he left the halfway house to visit his daughter. Seeing that the pickup truck of his wife's boyfriend was at the house, he flew into a rage. But "instead of acting on his impulse to carry a tire jack into the house to cause mayhem, he pulled out an instruction sheet with the tapping points and treated himself with an anger protocol until he was calm" (p. 61) and able to return to the center.

A comment by a therapist in one of the structured interviews paralleled many of the practitioner reports as she described a "dramatic shift … which would normally take years of therapy" (Mason, 2012, p. 227). A caution noted by several of the interviewees, however, is that the technique is being oversold in some of the materials promoting it. While believing that working with acupoints does indeed bring about faster change than the other methods at their disposal, the therapists noted that it is "not as rapid as the hype about energy psychology would suggest" (White, 2015, p. 43). This sets unrealistic expectations for clients and gives professionals reason to be suspicious. Although single session cures of longstanding phobias and other conditions have been documented and are not particularly uncommon, one of the interviewees quantified the change in treatment time since he introduced Energy Psychology into his practice. Prior to tapping, he estimated that he would spend up to four years working with childhood sexual abuse. Now he estimates that equivalent types of progress "can be completed in 6 months" (p. 43).

Breadth

In terms of the broad psychiatric categories that respond to Energy Psychology treatments, the majority of the 294 ACEP members completing the survey reported having experienced successes in treating some of the most common diagnoses, including generalized anxiety disorder, phobias, and depression (Feinstein, 2016). More than two thirds of the ACEP respondents reported success with PTSD. A 10-minute video illustrating an acupoint tapping approach in the rapid treatment of four combat veterans suffering with PTSD can be viewed at www.vetcases.com.

Nearly half of the respondents reported success with addictions, though only 3% felt they had any success at all in treating psychosis. Even with conditions that are deeply embedded in faulty neurochemistry, however, such as bipolar disorders or chronic schizophrenia, tapping treatments were able to reduce stress and help people cope more effectively. One therapist reported reductions in psychotic symptoms such as visual and auditory hallucinations.

It's not unusual for a therapy to shift focus from the initial reasons that treatment was being sought, but this often happens quite quickly with Energy Psychology. A medical doctor hadn't worked for five years because she was crippled with obsessive-compulsive disorder (OCD): "Walking along the street she'd be convinced that she bumped into an old person or a child, and she'd have to go back and find them. She couldn't drive [because] she'd become convinced that she'd knocked over a cyclist." Within a few sessions of EFT, her OCD symptoms had been eliminated and "she was back at work" (Chalmers, 2015, p. 32). Her life had been organized around her symptoms, and after the symptoms were cleared, her entire life constellation was transformed. While this is a dramatic example, many of the participants observed that reducing a person's symptoms or distress allows the natural ability for healing and rejuvenation to move forward. Once the body's stress chemicals "have been modulated, [this] allows you to negotiate with yourself and with the situation … in a rational and logical way" (Chalmers, 2015, p. 20).

Though this sequence holds for any successful psychotherapy, the way that the focus of the tapping can quickly move among emotions, sensations, memories, beliefs, behaviors, triggers, and concerns were seen as leading to outcomes that are more comprehensive than they are for many other therapeutic approaches. This flexibility, as well as the speed and precision with which tapping seems to shift the neurological underpinnings of whatever it targets, widens the scope of therapeutic outcomes.

An example from this author's own practice can provide greater detail than was usually found in the interviews. A woman who had heard that tapping can reduce reactions to invasive cancer treatments arranged for a series of Energy Psychology sessions concurrent with scheduled radiation treatments. Malignant masses had been found in her lymph nodes and at the base of her tongue, just above her vocal cords. She hoped to counter her strong fears about the treatment and modulate its side effects. Focusing at first on her fears and physical discomfort, it soon emerged that she was blaming herself for having gotten cancer. On questioning, she didn't believe that this was a particularly rational belief, but she nonetheless felt it strongly. I asked if she could remember other times that she was unfairly blamed. A powerful incident from her childhood immediately came to her mind. At age 10 she was held responsible for something terrible, but she was unable to defend herself because it would implicate others in the family. She was the active target of this unfounded blame for years, but she felt she couldn't speak up. Once the tapping eliminated the emotional charge carried around these painful experiences, a lifelong pattern of her not being able to tell her truths was explored and linked to these formative experiences. We then examined possible connections between her suppressed verbal expression ("shoving my truths down my throat," "keeping what I need to say under my tongue") and the subsequent cancer in the area of her throat, tongue, and vocal cords.

After each round of tapping, I asked her to imagine what was happening in her throat area as a quick gauge of the effects of that round. Then she would do another round of tapping, focusing on the images she was seeing in her throat at that point. She continued this tapping and imagery as homework. At first she saw heavy black tar and cobwebs. As the emotional charges on various aspects of the associated issues were lifted during the next two therapy sessions, the imagery changed until she had a sense of spaciousness and light moving through the area. The tar and cobwebs were gone. This corresponded with improvements in her CT scans that far exceeded her oncologist's expectations, particularly since she had discontinued radiation against his advice and also refused a recommended course of chemotherapy. Rather than increasing in size, all the masses had shrunk, some up to 50%. When she emailed me the results, she mentioned that she felt the tapping work was "instrumental." Meanwhile, her self-blame about having "given" herself cancer had transformed into self-compassion as she recognized the possible connections between her childhood situation and her illness. And her enhanced ability to express difficult truths led to a vivid new sense of empowerment.

Many of the therapists interviewed reported wide-ranging changes beyond the initial presenting problems. Another area where this theme was seen involved improved relationships with life partners, family members, friends, and colleagues. One of the therapists' clients explained that Energy Psychology helped improve relationships within her family because family members became "less reactive to one another" after having tapped on emotional triggers (Mason, 2012, p. 228).

Another therapist explained that insight without *repairing* early wounds, which is often an outcome of talk therapy, leads to "repeating entrenched patterns of interpersonal relating" as the wounds continually re-emerge (White, 2015, p. 33). Other changes mentioned which were tangential to the initial treatment goals included significant increases in confidence, self-esteem, assertiveness, mood, self-care, and capacity for emotional self-regulation. With more severe disorders, fewer self-harming behaviors and dissociative symptoms were reported (Schulz, 2009).

Several practitioners speculated that shifts at the emotional level *precede* changes in self-understanding, rather than the other way around, as is often the strategy of insight-oriented psychotherapies. A related dynamic identified by a number of the interviewees was that tapping on early issues can heal long-standing emotional injuries, while merely talking about them tends to embed unresolved formative experiences more deeply into the person's identity. As one of the interviewers summarized these observations: "talking increases 'identification with' or 'connection to' the trauma, whereas energy psychology clears the connection to the emotional and physiological charge associated with the trauma" (White, 2015, p. 36).

While most of these discussions focused on transformation in their clients' lives, a number of the therapists also disclosed that their own lives had undergone significant shifts since they began personally to apply tapping. One said it "saved her marriage" (White, 2015, p. 35). Many of the participants "attributed significant changes in their understanding of psychotherapeutic change, personal philosophy, and overall contentment in life to their experience of using energy psychology" (White, 2015, p. 5). A theme running through a number of the interviews was an increased sense of significance and gratification in their identity as therapists. This was characterized by one of the interviewers as *living one's life purpose*: "This might be described as feeling passionate about what you are doing, engaged, loving what you are doing, feeling that there's nothing else you want to be doing, living in the moment when you are doing it, feeling joyous and fulfilled" (Chalmers, 2015, p. 29). A seasoned therapist, who was past retirement age but still had a thriving practice, noted that since introducing Energy Psychology, he was again "excited by" his work (White, 2015, p. 35). Another felt a sense of special accomplishment: "I'm doing something of great value by helping the person to break through their fears" (Chalmers, 2015, p. 29).

Safety

The risk of retraumatizing people while attempting to help them overcome PTSD or other emotional wounds following abuse, warfare, serious accidents, assaults, or exposure to traumatic events is one of the ongoing hazards for trauma therapists (Duckworth & Follette, 2011). Acupoint tapping protocols seem less vulnerable to this risk. Tapping protocols "are designed to approach distress in a graduated and tolerable way, titrating exposure to otherwise unbearable trauma that may have previously overwhelmed the client's coping capacities" (Mollon, 2013, p. 355). A review of clinical trials of Energy Psychology treatments involving more than a thousand subjects found that no "adverse events" were reported (Church, 2013). The interviews with the 12 psychologists working with adult survivors of childhood sexual abuse reported that Energy Psychology allows their clients to "relieve the trauma in a non-invasive manner [that] lessens the possibility of retraumatization" (Schulz, 2009, p. 17).

Tapping practitioners were seen as having an advantage in their ability to modulate the amount of distress clients experience, to keep them within what is called the "window of tolerance"

(Corrigan et al., 2011). This is the zone in which enough engagement with the traumatic event is established as to allow healing to occur while at the same time not overwhelming the person. Energy Psychology is able to keep people within this zone by shifting activity if the person begins to become uncomfortably aroused or distressed. Attention can immediately change to calming the physiological responses by bringing the focus of the tapping to these somatic experiences *while* they are occurring. The therapists participating in the surveys and interviews portrayed Energy Psychology as a "safe and gentle intervention" (Mason, 2012, p. 228) with "a very low incidence of decompensation or abreaction when working with traumatic material" (White, 2015, p. 44).

The major reason reported for people not being helped, and perhaps being harmed from an Energy Psychology treatment, wasn't due to the treatment itself, according to a few of the respondents, but rather because of practitioners who do not "have the skills required to manage the complex relational dynamics that sometimes emerge in the treatment of trauma" (White, 2015, p. 37). If revisiting a traumatic memory brings up overwhelming feelings, for instance, and the practitioner doesn't know how to bring the client back into the window of tolerance, the entire experience may be retraumatizing and also diminish confidence in the ability of any psychotherapy to be safe and of genuine help. These issues become more critical as life coaches and others trained in Energy Psychology protocols but not in other areas of mental health—such as how to work with dissociation, suicidality, psychosis, severe depression, et cetera—have been offering services to the general public. Major psychiatric disorders need to be recognized and referrals made as appropriate.

A perplexing issue is that as clients learn to tap on a self-help basis, they may utilize the power of the technique in the service of self-defeating beliefs or self-concepts that are at the core of the problems for which they are seeking treatment. For instance, in an email exchange with other tapping therapists about working with eating disorders, psychologist Peta Stapleton wrote: "I am hesitant to use EFT for patients in the throes of anorexia nervosa as they sometimes use it to reduce hunger… . I prefer to use it when recovery is underway and we can use it for anxiety over meals and weight gain." This astute caution also applies for the treatment of other conditions in which the client might use tapping in the service of self-destructive impulses or perceptions.

Another delicate consideration in using acupoint tapping pointed out by a couple of the interviewees is that it is so powerful that "one can go too deeply, too quickly" (Mason, 2012, p. 229). Transformational change "means that we are no longer the person we knew" (p. 231). Particularly for people who are emotionally unstable, any potent intervention, no matter how beneficial it may seem, can be disorienting. Even relaxation techniques can paradoxically increase anxiety levels (Heide & Borkovec, 1984). People may need more support than is obvious "to pace and tolerate rapid changes" (p. 231). As one of the therapists put it, "Like with anything, you have to pay attention to the impact" (p. 229). It may be more important, for instance, to first help the client build ego strength and a strong therapeutic alliance than to dive into long-standing problems, particularly those that arise from traumatic experiences. Yet overall, most of the therapists described an unusually "low level of adverse effects experienced from the use of energy psychology [even with clients] who can often be fragile" (p. 229).

Therapeutic Alliance

The quality of the "therapeutic alliance" that is established between a client and a therapist is a strong predictor of the success of the therapy (Ardito & Rabellino, 2011). Therapeutic alliance refers to the degree to which the client and the therapist are engaged in "collaborative, purposive work" that addresses the client's reasons for being in treatment (Bordin, 1979, p. 293). This transcends the therapist's theoretical orientation. One of the interviewers observed that the participants emphasized the degree to which Energy Psychology treatments involve "a creative process within the relationship" (Mason, 2012, p. 229). While Energy Psychology can be self-applied, working with a practitioner can often take the process deeper and into more aspects of the person's life. In systematic interviews with 16 seasoned therapists who introduced EFT into their existing practices, all reported that it enhanced their therapeutic alliance with their clients (Nairn, 2020). Their speculations on the reasons for this included:

1. Their clients experienced rapid, ongoing, tangible, even if small, shifts that

constituted subjective proof that the therapy was working.
2. Seeing the therapist tap along with the client demonstrated the therapist's engagement, resulting in the client feeling a greater sense of "togetherness."
3. The therapist's self-tapping on the client's issues was experienced by the therapists as enhancing their intuition about those issues.
4. The addition of coordinated physical movement introduced a ritualistic quality that brought the therapist and client into greater alignment.

Excerpts from the interviews showed the therapists also attempting to articulate a less tangible dimension that was added by working with the body and its "energetic field." As one of them put it: "Once you start working with energy … it changes the relationship… . It brings you together in an energetic loop which is very different [from] psychotherapeutic distance" (Nairn, 2020, p. 63).

Enhanced Intuitive Access

Whether an "energetic loop" is established or it is simply that intuition is somehow expanded when using acupoint tapping protocols, many of the practitioners interviewed reported such a shift after they introduced Energy Psychology into their practices: their ability to find the right words and understanding for the clinical moment, without relying on conscious reasoning, seemed to increase. One of them described how "sometimes I feel like I'm on a roll flying with intuition and input … I have no idea where these ideas are coming from but wow, they work" (Chalmers, 2015, p. 31).

Many of the tapping therapists in the interview studies made some reference to this sort of attunement occurring during their tapping sessions. One interviewer characterized such experiences as being when therapist and client are "in the flow" (Chalmers, 2015). While recognizing that "it is difficult to know whether this is intuition or very well-developed observation skills," she noted that the common ingredient is a sense of "receiving information from another place" (p.30). One of the therapists she interviewed described how he empathetically feels what his clients are feeling:

> Sometimes I'll be partway through a session and I'll say, "Do you have a headache?" Or, "Has your neck gone tight?' Nine out of ten times they'll say, "Yeah, just went tight just then." And they'll say, "How do you know?" And I'll say, "Well I'm feeling it." (p. 32)

Another expressed "surprise at what comes out":

> Where on earth did that come from? You know, things come to you [that] have a profound effect on the client. Afterwards you think, "That was clever, how did I get to that point, or what made me say that?" And you've got absolutely no idea… . All I know is that it works, and if you go with the flow, it can yield some fantastic results. (p. 30)

Another described how productive these experiences can be:

> When you're in rapport with the client, it's as if you're in a bubble with them and the whole world goes away … and that's when the magic begins to happen… . That's when things begin to open up [to] the roots of their problem. (p. 30)

Yet another talked about her respect for intuitive insights and the way they can shorten the time required to process a complex issue:

> The information that comes through seems to be true quite often. It's remarkable. I can often ask a question and the client will say, "How did you know?" How did I know? I don't know how I knew. I just knew, and a jump like that can save you hours of verbal processing because you're jumping from one level to another very, very quickly. It cuts out all the processing in between. (pp. 31–32)

One of the therapists was doing a demonstration session at a conference while attached to an EEG brain-wave monitor. The person operating the monitor turned to her and said, "You don't know what you're doing!" The therapist elaborated, "By that she meant when I was working, there were very, very few brainwaves of conscious thought. The brainwaves she was seeing in me were the deeper subconscious, unconscious brainwaves" (p. 31).

Another therapist reflected on whether the information is coming from her own mind or from somewhere beyond it. Here is how she distinguishes between the two:

> There does come a point in a session where information starts coming from somewhere else.

> I just know what the next question is to ask, or I can sense what they are feeling or thinking. It's hard to say where it's coming from, but with practice you get a definable sense of "this is right." If something is coming from my own mind or experiences, there's a different feel to it. (p. 31)

Most psychotherapists, regardless of modality, sense or acknowledge that intuition plays a role in their clinical work (Stickle & Arnd-Caddigan, 2019). Whether or not this is more so for Energy Psychology practitioners, many of those interviewed felt their intuition became sharper after they began to work at an energetic level, almost as if attuning to energy provided an opening into the intuitive realm. Of 149 therapists responding to an online survey, the 42% who reported using or being inclined to use energy treatments were more likely than the others to rely on their intuition in their decision-making and their choice of treatment methods, and they trusted intuitive insight more than conventional forms of critical thinking (Gaudiano et al., 2012). While Gaudiano et al. saw this as a weakness in the practitioners, these findings can be interpreted both ways.

A therapist in one of the interviews described how she is able to sense when a client's energy changes by a change in her own energy: "In that moment of their shifting, my energy shifts too" (Chalmers, 2015, p. 31). From such a felt shift in the therapist's *energies*, different words, insights, or directions seem to follow "intuitively."

Spiritual Attunement

To the degree that psychotherapists believe their discipline grows out of science and medicine, spiritual matters have been relegated to the metaphysical, mystical, or religious, and largely disregarded. But spiritual concerns are intimately entwined with the human psyche. In fact, a "relationship between spirituality and mental health has been widely demonstrated by many different investigators over the years all around the world, usually showing lower rates of drug use, lower prevalence of depression and suicidal attempts and better quality of life and well being" (Damiano et al., 2016, p. 11). This relationship also extends into physical health, including "less hospitalization, better coping with the disease, better treatment adherence, more acceptance of therapeutic measures, and lower mortality rates" (p. 11). Damiano et al. describe spirituality as "the personal quest for understanding answers to ultimate questions about life, about meaning and about relationship to the sacred or transcendent" (p. 11). Some therapists use the term *nature* to describe the intelligent forces behind the workings of the universe and *unconscious* to describe the demonstrated intelligence that is beyond the grasp of the conscious mind. Others use terms such as "Spirit" and "soul." Whatever the terms they use, however, many therapists have come to recognize a relationship between the deepest realms of the human psyche and mental health. As summarized in an article in the *Journal of Religion and Health*: "Problems of the soul cannot be reduced to symptoms of psychological ill health" (Berghash & Jillson, 1998, p. 313).

The tapping practitioners interviewed were generally judged by the interviewers as having "a well-developed sense of compassion and spirituality" (Chalmers, 2015, p. 27). The practitioners felt that "energy work could help them connect with clients on a spiritual level, which they felt enabled deeper healing" (Mason, 2012, p. 230). While they were "not searching for an approach for spiritual realization" (White, 2015, p. 41), they believed their spirituality had become more pronounced based on their work in Energy Psychology. As with the use of intuition, it is not known whether tapping therapists experience this sense of spiritual harmony more than other psychotherapists, but some felt this attunement with the body's energies may be a portal into these realms. One of the interviewers reflected that for several of the practitioners, it was like "going beyond physical and psychological presence … drawing from universal energy" (White, 2015, p. 49). The spiritual dimension of tapping work for one of the therapists was characterized by the interviewer as an "*energetic* … she experiences but cannot name or fully articulate" (White, 2015, p. 41). Another therapist reflected, "I connect to the wider field, and I let it all flow through me" (Chalmers, 2015, p. 30). Another said, "I work with being open to input from the universe" (Chalmers, 2015, p. 30). One of the interviewers noted that the sense of deepening spirituality among the practitioners was associated not only with peace, oneness, and expanded consciousness, but also with "a letting go of a need for certainty … greater comfort with unknowns" (White, 2015, p. 41).

When speaking of spirituality, several of the therapists "consistently referred to the importance of therapeutic presence in Energy Psychology" (White, 2015, p. 38). This need not be defined in mystical or religious terms. Explaining his personal experience of therapeutic presence, Carl Rogers, one of the most influential psychologists of the 20th century, reflected:

> When I am closest to my inner intuitive self ... when I can relax and be close to the transcendental core of me ... it seems that my inner spirit has reached out and touched the inner spirit of the other. Our relationship transcends itself and becomes a part of something larger. Profound growth and healing and energy are present. (Rogers, 1980, p. 129)

A number of the tapping therapists expressed similar thoughts. Tapping protocols bring both practitioner and client into a mindful process, a "witnessing attitude" that is attuned to the body's ever-shifting energy states (White, 2015, p. 40). As with meditation, among the most widely reported outcomes of Energy Psychology treatments is a marked reduction in distress. One of the interviewers noted that all of the participants described "how their capacity for presence increased as their underlying fears, anxieties, and neurotic tendencies decreased" after applying Energy Psychology to their own issues (White, 2015, p. 39). Explaining that something "bigger than herself" is evoked during her sessions, one of the therapists said: "There is a deeper connection going on, and in that connection, we are all one" (Chalmers, 2015, p. 27). Others also spoke of a "feeling of oneness" during their work with clients (Chalmers, 2015, p. 30). One of the therapists was unequivocal in characterizing her therapy as entering a spiritual domain: "I work on a spiritual level. My job is to try as much as possible to get out of the way" (Chalmers, 2015, p. 30). The therapists generally described this deepening spirituality in terms of "experiencing spirituality rather than believing in some spiritual construct or philosophy" (White, 2015, p. 40).

Reflections from Clients

The surveys and interviews discussed above were based largely on the practitioners' observations about their clients. So while the accounts of rapid outcomes, transformational change, safety, and a strong therapeutic alliance are generalizations about their clients' experiences, most of the reports were not in the words of the clients themselves.

A study that did capture clients' words involved interviews with eight individuals who used a tapping protocol for help with a physical disease (Kalla et al., 2020). Two had self-applied the method and the other six were guided by a practitioner. The interviewees reported three types of issues that frequently emerged and were successfully addressed by acupoint tapping: (a) the role of unresolved emotional issues in their illness, (b) outdated beliefs and self-defeating behavioral patterns that were contributing factors in the genesis and maintenance of the illness, and (c) ways the illness was serving as a buffer from the expectations of others. All eight participants came to recognize that unresolved emotional issues played a role in their illness. For instance, a woman who had suffered with arthritis for years described this experience:

> My husband passed away almost 20 years ago. My children were really young at that time. So there was really no time to stop and feel grief. And realizing that it was all those emotions that had been locked up. The lower back pain ... . was gone in like one major session that we did. The pain was gone. It was like literally gone [laughs]. It was emotions and attachment that was holding in the back. Overnight when it cleared, I was like, "Oh my God!" you know, "it's just gone!" (p. 219)

Although Kalla et al. (2020) is the only study to date presenting systematic interviews with tapping clients, hundreds of descriptions of the experiences of people who have benefitted from tapping in working with a wide range of issues are posted on the internet (many can be found on www.EFTUniverse.com, www.emofree.com, and www.EFTInternational.org). Beyond anecdotal reports, more than a hundred clinical trials have tracked symptoms and other measures before and after tapping treatments. While these studies consistently report strong, rapid, and durable outcomes (Feinstein, 2021), our focus here is on how Energy Psychology is *experienced* by the people who use it. To obtain fresh first-person accounts, several colleagues who use acupoint tapping were asked by the current author to identify a client they were able to help after other therapies had not been as successful.

The clients who were identified were then asked to respond to questions designed to elicit comparisons between the approaches. Their responses matched themes that are found on the web-posted reports. One theme was the way the insights and reminders about faulty thinking produced by psychodynamic and cognitive treatments were judged as less helpful than the rapid changes in the emotional landscape underlying the issues of concern brought about by the tapping therapies. For instance, a woman who had undergone several years of conventional talk therapy reflected:

> Talking therapy helped me understand what my issues were. Before this process, I lived with an overall sense of sadness and hopelessness, without really knowing where it was coming from, or how to solve it. Psychotherapy helped me understand where I was blocked, where I was fearful, and mostly, where I was divided. Even if this was enriching, intellectual understanding of the cause of my suffering was not enough to set me free. I spent uncountable sessions running in circles, hoping for freedom, but never quite getting there.

After her Energy Psychology sessions, she described how:

> I felt like a new layer of these issues was being reached. The tapping felt like a laser beaming directly into my blockages. I witnessed the speed and effectiveness of the tapping exercises. I felt that "something" shifted after every round of tapping, making me feel lighter and freer every time.

Another frequent theme was how useful it is to be able to self-apply tapping whenever the need arises. A woman whose profession requires her to present public seminars had suffered from generalized anxiety disorder (GAD). She had:

> … spent years in various therapies. When I got introduced to tapping, my life changed. I had been overreacting and getting overwhelmed to just about everything. That is not true anymore because I can tap whenever anything new comes up. Particularly amazing was my lifetime battle with public speaking, which does not exist anymore.

Yet another theme involved the way that once a problem has been overcome, it tends not to return. A psychotherapist described how this has worked for her personally:

> CBT [Cognitive Behavior Therapy], DBT [Dialectical Behavior Therapy], and Mindfulness need to be practiced repeatedly. With EFT, once something is treated, it is usually gone permanently. Further work on the issue isn't needed.

The presenting problems ranged from overcoming blocks about completing a graduate thesis to severe psychiatric conditions. For instance, a 56-year-old woman had been diagnosed with dissociative identity disorder, chronic PTSD, and major depressive disorder. She was formally designated as "permanently disabled." She had gone through years of therapy with numerous practitioners as well as several psychiatric hospitalizations. She described the "exposure" therapies she had experienced:

> Prior to utilizing tapping and related energy psychology methods, previous therapists followed the "re-experience the trauma until it isn't such a hot memory" desensitization type of therapies with disastrous results for me personally. I was continually encouraged to search my memories to force myself to recall painful incidents. This type of therapy caused me great distress and increased the frequency and severity of my dissociative episodes.

She describes how this changed after she began working with a therapist who uses Energy Psychology:

> Tapping allowed me to self-regulate and process as opposed to being flooded. It allowed me to explore memories while still feeling safe, at my own pace. It allowed me to become consciously aware of all aspects of myself. I am able to revisit memories from a safe distance without internalizing the highly charged emotions associated with past traumas.
>
> The single biggest difference was my ability to function after each session. Prior therapies triggered me tremendously, and I lacked an effective safety net to deal with the fallout from that on my own. With tapping, I was able to stabilize with less fear and less abreaction each time, moving forward incrementally. I felt a greater sense of personal

> control with tapping. Another huge benefit was the ability to eliminate all psychiatric medications, which meant eliminating the debilitating side effects from those medications.

She summarized:

> Traditional therapy and medications may be helpful to some, but for me they compounded the problem. The more "help" I received, the more my life spiraled out of control. They left me feeling hopeless and worthless and deepened my levels of guilt, worthlessness, and shame. Tapping and energy psychology techniques allowed me to process the traumas and really start to heal without creating more dysfunction. I find it empowering and motivating. Tapping has helped me love myself and continue to strive to be my best whole self.

Another comparison of conventional therapy vs. Energy Psychology treatments for a serious psychiatric disorder came from a man who had been on disability for clinical depression. He described his disappointment with previous therapists as a "waste of time … Not one offered me any way to deal with the issues I was having." In his first Energy Psychology session, the therapist "offered tapping techniques to alleviate stress and physical pain" caused by a medical condition. He "immediately felt calm, and my pain, which I experienced for years, was reduced to 2 out of 10 where it had been 7." In subsequent sessions, he was also "given tapping tools to manage stress and anxiety." He reports that when he started with Energy Psychology, he "was very dysfunctional. I thought of suicide many times a day. I found it difficult to perform daily tasks, find words in conversations, or maintain a train of thought for very long at all. Now I may have a fleeting thought of suicide, but I do not give it a moment's attention. Tapping turned my pain and discomfort from unbearable to very manageable." He has also returned to gainful employment.

Guidelines for Practice

The interviews and surveys involving more than 800 Energy Psychology practitioners, along with the direct reports from clients, hold implications for the use of acupoint tapping as a tool for emotional healing. While many of the insights that were offered apply to all forms of psychotherapy—such as building solid rapport and conducting appropriate assessments—a summary of those that are specific to Energy Psychology follows. They fell into the categories of Treatment Focus, Use of Language, Resonance, Time Orientation, Cautions, Resistance to Tapping, Countertransference, Self-Help Applications, and Integrating Energy Psychology with Other Techniques.

Treatment Focus

The therapists who were interviewed uniformly discussed their use of tapping for the resolution of longstanding emotional issues, but the range of targeted outcomes also included work on marital difficulties, physical challenges, and performance goals. Whatever the target, however, practitioners emphasized the importance of helping clients become attuned to their "body language, voice tone, and energy [as well as] sights, sounds, smells, physical sensations, and thoughts" (Stapleton, 2019, p. 89). Complex problems were separated into parts that could then be individually addressed at their emotional and somatic roots with the acupoint tapping.

The importance of being highly specific (e.g., "the smell of his breath") rather than general or vague (e.g., "that bad thing that happened") was emphasized by many of the practitioners. The notable exception is when strategically minimizing the chances of retraumatization with a fragile client, in which case statements such as *that bad thing that happened* might be well-calibrated, allowing "clients to slowly sneak in on their issues" (Stapleton, 2019, p. 104) while remaining within their window of tolerance. The practitioners also "discussed ways in which they may 'ease' their clients" into the therapy process by starting with "surface-level issues" (Kalla et al., 2018, p. 1668).

The level of specificity sometimes employed during tapping sessions may in some cases seem excessive, yet tapping on every available aspect of an issue can ensure a more complete and permanent resolution. In a dramatic instance, a man who had suffered a stroke was told by his doctor that the paralyzed left side of his body would never recover. The practitioner reported working in minute detail, such as putting the man's fingers in the needed positions for various tasks, while she herself tapped on the man's acupoints, suggesting wordings such as "my arm remembers, my hand remembers, and my cells in my arm remember how to do this" (Kalla et al., 2018, p. 19). He was then able to hold small objects, including a pen. But he couldn't write with it. After tapping to bring back the ability to write, he "managed to write a few words" (p. 19). This was all within an hour. In this manner he was able to "undertake specific tasks incrementally" (p. 20). By the next visit he was able to pick up a mobile phone. Feelings and motion also began to return to his left leg. The therapist was quite moved: "It was a bit surreal because it all happened so quickly" (p. 20). While Energy Psychology most often addresses emotional as well as somatic aspects of an issue, the interviewer reflected on how "without appearing to investigate emotional issues," the therapist guided "her client to engage with his physical body" in a way that quickly began to restore greater control (p. 20).

Tapping sessions were often guided by following what is sometimes called the client's *emotion and thought trail.* Even though the practitioners might have an idea of where the work is headed, they also emphasized the importance of staying attuned to the client's pace and direction, "starting wherever the client is" (Chalmers, 2015, p. 25). As one of the interviewers summarized this, Energy Psychology teaches "the therapist to stand back [and] prioritize clients' present moment experience" (White, 2015, p. 48). Another noted, "It may be with something apparently small, but this is not for the practitioner to judge" (Chalmers, 2015, p. 25). This requires becoming "comfortable with ambiguity ... with not knowing what's going to emerge" (Chalmers, 2015, p. 26). Another interviewer emphasized that letting the client lead applies "regardless of the apparent connection or lack thereof, to the target issue" (Kalla et al., 2018, p. 1659) All this includes "holding the space" (Chalmers, 2015, p. 26) for past trauma or other aversive childhood events to emerge at the client's own pace. While the practitioner certainly fosters the process, several of the interviewees mentioned how important it is not to impose the therapist's agenda.

Use of Language

The therapists interviewed frequently mentioned, in one way or another, that an important element of the work involves "formulating the right words" (Mason, 2012, p. 228). Some of the therapists placed a premium on using a client's exact words when possible as the statements to repeat while tapping. One of them explained how using the words of her clients is a way of "reaching into their subconscious" (Chalmers, 2015, p. 20). Using the client's exact wording evokes very specific experiences and meanings that keep the therapy on target. Nonetheless, crafting tapping phrases that move a session forward is an important part of the art of delivery during Energy Psychology treatments. A study of videotaped sessions identified 62 therapeutic functions that can be served by the wordings the client originates or repeats while tapping, all falling within the broad categories of "attuning," "exploring," or "leading." (Feinstein, 2019, p. 41).

Beyond the words, however, a strength of acupoint tapping is that it can produce strong desired effects without any words so long as the person is inwardly attuned to the issue of concern. A recent brain imaging study found that stimulating acupoints while viewing unpleasant images not only made the experience of looking at the images become less aversive, the activation of brain regions involved with negative feelings also shifted (Wittfoth et al., 2020). This is particularly useful in early work with trauma survivors who may not even be capable of describing their ordeals (Hamne & Sandstrom, 2014). The therapists interviewed seemed to agree that tapping can facilitate a desensitization to trauma without the need for talking about the traumatic experience. As one of the interviewers summarized it, Energy Psychology is an important treatment option for clients who "are at risk of decompensation due to flooding of traumatic material" (White, 2015, p. 5).

Tapping may also be applied without any understanding of the underlying mechanisms of action. Nor is age a barrier. One of the therapists described a child who had to regularly endure a painful procedure as part of his ongoing medical treatment for a serious illness: "He taps. His parents ask, 'Why are you doing this?' He goes, 'Because it hurts less.' He doesn't need to understand it" (Kalla et al., 2018, p. 21). As one of the tapping therapists described the process of methodically working with traumatized individuals: "We clear one trauma away and another one pops up and we clear that" (White, 2015, p. 36).

What the words add, with their 62 identified functions, is an ability to guide the client through layer after layer of complex issues with unusual speed, clarity, and precision (Feinstein, 2019). Words provide bridges between the mind and the body that seem to combine with tapping to facilitate deep and rapid change.

Resonance

More than 80 years ago, Rollo May observed that "both the counselor and the counselee are taken out of themselves and become merged in a common psychic entity. The emotions and will of each become part of this new psychic entity" (May, 1989[1939], p. 67). One of May's students, Virginia Larson, a psychologist who studied this "new psychic entity," described a striking incident from her own clinical work:

> A new client entered my office for the first appointment. I spontaneously began experiencing very subtle, unusual sensations in my own lower torso. Prior to this appointment I had completed a deep relaxation exercise, so I was quite aware when the subtle, tingly sensations began. I first reflected inwardly trying to discover the source of the mysterious sensations. I asked myself if the new client reminded me of someone I had previously known. I searched myself to ascertain if my own personal memories were related to the tingly sensations. Then I bracketed the experience noting it, watching it, and reflecting further upon it. Finally, my curiosity was overpowering. At a seemingly appropriate point, I described my experience to the young woman client, and asked if my experience had some meaning for her. The young woman immediately replied, "Oh yes, I have cancer of the cervix, and I've been having chemotherapy there." (Larson, 1987, p. 323)

Investigating this phenomenon, which she termed "psychotherapeutic resonance," Larson found that many therapists report a momentary merging of the boundary between themselves and a client that in its intensity and the reach of its understanding exceeds empathy and rapport.

"Matching a client's pace, mirroring their body language, and tapping with a client" (Chalmers, 2015, p. 23) were all mentioned as ways of increasing resonance and building rapport. The very structure of Energy Psychology protocols, which require close, evident, uninterrupted attunement, keeps the practitioner "in the moment [rather than] thinking about what's happening next … about what you are going to do for dinner … about the things going on in your own life" (Chalmers, 2015, p. 26).

Another way of staying attuned to the client's experience is to have them "check the SUD [Subjective Units of Distress] rating regularly" (Stapleton, 2019, p. 90). This provides immediate feedback that influences the next step in the treatment. Simple physical attunements can also keep the treatment aligned with the client's experience, such as adjusting the pace of the tapping. Tapping too rapidly "may feed into the anxiety loop" of people who are anxious (Stapleton, 2019, p. 90), while initially using slow tapping with depressed clients "will match their energy state" (Stapleton, 2019, p. 104).

Time Orientation

The therapists were in agreement that tapping can be oriented around events from the *past*, can focus on emotions surrounding a *present* concern, or can address fears, misgivings, or desired outcomes for the *future*. Treatment with a new client typically begins with identifying and addressing present-day concerns. The therapists reported that these might be self-defeating behaviors, beliefs, or emotional response patterns that are currently active, but also that "it almost always ends up going a lot deeper … penetrating into earlier childhood experiences" (Kalla et al., 2018, p. 1669). Early events may be introduced spontaneously by the client or come from the therapist's intuition or questioning. In later stages of treatment—after emotional wounds have been attended, longstanding issues have been addressed, and self-defeating beliefs countered—triggers and complications that are likely to come up in the future are anticipated. These become a focus until the tapping has substantially reduced their emotional grip. Then the way is clear for envisioning and tapping on best possible futures. Of course where the treatment will initially focus depends on the client's readiness. Evoking the "first" or "worst memory" involving the target symptom can move things along very quickly if the client is emotionally prepared and the therapeutic alliance well established (Stapleton, 2019). In practice, sessions may move quite facilely amongst past, present, and future, giving the approach a "time machine" quality.

Cautions

Staying within one's "scope of practice" is an important consideration for anyone offering psychological services. In a survey completed by 22 EFT therapists, adequate training for delivering the type of service being offered was emphasized.

For instance, practitioners who work with traumatized clients need to understand dissociation and how to "handle abreactions well if they occur" (Stapleton & Chatwin, 2017, p. 16). In formulating treatment plans and setting directions, several practitioners cautioned that therapists both accept a client's personal limits and recognize the client as a "whole person" rather than a diagnostic category (Stapleton & Chatwin, 2017, p. 16). Appreciating the client "as an active self-healer ... possessing his/her own wisdom" was also emphasized (Kalla et al., 2018, p. 1659).

Treatment guidelines for using Energy Psychology with trauma survivors were derived from a survey completed by 448 EFT practitioners (Church et al., 2017). Two-thirds of the practitioners reported that "more than 60% of PTSD clients are fully rehabilitated, and 89% stated that less than 10% of clients make little or no progress" (p. 16). The guidelines were formulated from an analysis of the therapist's answers within the context of existing PTSD research literature and best PTSD practices recommendations. They were further developed in a subsequent presentation (Church et al., 2018). In terms of cautions, the guidelines show a deep respect for the psychological potency of traumatic experiences. They "recommend a stepped-care model, with five treatment sessions for subclinical PTSD, 10 sessions for PTSD, and escalation to intensive psychotherapy or psychopharmacology or both for nonresponsive patients and those with developmental trauma" (Church et al., 2018, p. 146). Throughout the treatment, clients are encouraged to also use online self-help resources, social support, and group therapy.

Resistance to Tapping

Many of the practitioners interviewed or surveyed in the studies recognized that tapping on the body looks strange and doesn't seem to make much sense according to conventional ways of thinking. Use of the word "energy" is also confusing to both the public and professionals, allowing the method to be more readily discounted (Mitchell & Chatzidamianos, 2020). In the words of one of the interviewers, "The concept of an energy system is perhaps the most controversial aspect of the work within the prevailing paradigms" (Mason, 2012, p. 231). On the other hand, the rapidly growing research base and more rigorous training programs are helping shift these opinions (Mitchell & Chatzidamianos, 2020). The growing use of acupoint tapping, along with word-of-mouth descriptions of rapid success with difficult diagnoses, also lend credibility to the approach. Nonetheless, finesse is required in introducing it into the treatment setting. Tapping on the skin as a way of shifting emotional difficulties may seem so counterintuitive that no form of persuasion is going to be effective until the client has personally experienced a positive outcome.

For instance, while the reports of EFT in correctional settings mentioned earlier described striking improvements, an initial phase of resistance to the approach was consistently encountered. The prisoners were skeptical when EFT was explained, some saying it looked "ridiculous and laughable." Inmates became more accepting, however, as the frequent use of the 0-to-10 SUD scale gave them a sense of hope because it helped register that change was indeed occurring. Another step in overcoming their resistance involved their realization that "they would not have to talk and recount what they had said repeatedly to others." An obstacle to eventually going deeper, however, was that the male inmates in particular were often "reluctant to discuss emotions or personal situations, which in their minds would reveal weakness." This was countered as the focus shifted "from working on negative issues to inviting the young men and women to consider dreams, goals, and life objectives, using the tapping to strengthen" these aspirations (Hartung & Morales, 2019, pp. 58–59).

Countertransference

Countertransference, a term coined by Freud, describes the way therapists unconsciously project their feelings and unresolved conflicts onto the client. The therapist's emotional response to a client may be informative about the client's issues, but when the therapy becomes a trigger for the therapist's unhealed wounds, the relationship may become confusing, unproductive, or even harmful. Just the intimate attunement, particularly to a client's pain and suffering, may weigh heavily on any therapist and also activate unresolved emotional issues. These effects may be magnified when attuning to clients at an energetic level. The interviewees described how they use tapping outside the client sessions to modulate their reactions. One of the interviewers summarized: "Practitioners are clear that they face challenges when a client's issue triggers them and that they need to keep working on themselves to reduce these reactions" (Chalmers, 2015, p. 28). Another interviewer noted that "using EFT personally after sessions with very distressed clients helped to reduce the impact of counter-transference" (Mason, 2012, p. 230). Beyond emphasizing the need to be aware of their own biases, countertransference, and boundaries, responses to a question about the qualities of an effective Energy Psychology practitioner included that the person regularly use the practice in "his/her own life." (Stapleton & Chatwin, 2017, p. 16).

Self-Help Applications

The number of individuals who have applied Energy Psychology on a self-help basis is likely in the tens of millions. Traffic on the top five EFT websites has been tracked using a statistical tool that showed more than six million visits during a randomly selected month (Church et al., 2014). The 12th annual online World Tapping Summit, held during the last week of February 2020, attracted more than 600,000 participants (personal communication, Nick Ortner, August 4, 2020). A mobile app that guides users in applying acupoint tapping protocols for anxiety and stress was investigated in a large-scale study including 270,461 app users and found highly significant ($p < 0.001$) symptom reduction (Church et al., 2020).

Practitioners responding to one of the surveys highlighted the value of "teaching the client to tap on day-to-day triggers … Tapping on any thoughts or feelings related to worries and anxieties about future situations was also recommended" (Stapleton, 2019, p. 89). While "clients often reported that the techniques were more powerful during a session than when clients used them on their own" (Mason, 2012, p. 230), the experience of being able to manage their feelings, thoughts and reactions on a self-help basis not only advanced the goals of the therapy, it was self-empowering in other areas of their lives as well. Giving "tapping homework" to their clients was frequently mentioned.

Integrating Energy Psychology with Other Techniques

A trait of effective Energy Psychology practitioners, as identified by some of the survey respondents, is that they are "creative" in combining tapping with other strategies and approaches (Stapleton & Chatwin, 2017, p. 16). Certain techniques that fall outside of Energy Psychology protocols per se are frequently utilized, such as *diaphragmatic breathing*, *grounding*, *mindfulness*, *guided imagery*, the *daily energy routine* from energy medicine (Eden, 2008), *visualizing a safe place* (Stapleton, 2019, p. 90), the *empty chair technique* from Gestalt therapy (Polster & Polster, 1974), *parts work* (Schwartz, 2021), and the *affect bridge* from hypnosis (Watkins, 1971). Two thirds of the licensed mental health professionals in the ACEP survey integrated Energy Psychology protocols into their existing practices" (Feinstein, 2016, p. 37). Many of them used tapping within the context of cognitive, psychodynamic, and other talk-oriented modalities. Although most of the practitioners integrated Energy Psychology within other theoretical frameworks, some found it useful to "distinguish talk therapy and Energy Psychology as two separate paradigms" (White, 2015, p. 35). While somatic interventions such as acupoint tapping were believed by the practitioners to be markedly faster and more effective than talk therapy alone, the interviewees also appreciated that "sometimes clients need a space to talk about their experience" (White, 2015, p. 37).

Limitations

Of the thousands of observations presented in the studies that were the source for this paper, the selection of the statements emphasized was based on those that resonated with this paper's author. Although he is an experienced Energy Psychology practitioner and researcher who over the past two decades has had in-depth discussions with hundreds of Energy Psychology practitioners (face-to-face or electronically), no attempt was made to utilize systematic, interactive appraisal standards that rely on a panel of experts, such as the Delphi method (Linstone & Turoff, 1975). While this review attempted to represent the data accurately and in a useful manner, the author's biases are inevitably woven into the discussion. The practitioners who were interviewed or surveyed also had a favorable bias toward Energy Psychology in that their participation in the study was predicated on their professional identification with the method. Also, even 800 is a relatively small sampling of the tens of thousands of therapists estimated to be using at least some Energy Psychology techniques. The source studies also varied in their academic rigor and sampling methods, so this investigation is more an informed selection of the views of the individuals who participated in the studies than an objective, comprehensive, highly systematic analysis attempting to reflect impartially the opinions of the entire Energy Psychology practitioner community.

Conclusion

More than 800 therapists, counselors, or life coaches who use Energy Psychology methods on a professional basis have participated in online surveys or systematic interviews in 15 separate studies focusing on various aspects of the practice. From these studies, this paper has identified and explored six general themes. The practitioners reported that, in relation to other methods at their disposal, Energy Psychology protocols led to more rapid outcomes in the treatment of a wide range of psychological conditions, less likelihood of retraumatizing clients, a stronger therapeutic alliance, enhanced access to personal intuition, and a bridge into greater spiritual attunement. Nine guidelines for the effective application of Energy Psychology methods were also derived and discussed. All of which leads to a final distilled conclusion: Practitioners are encouraged to draw upon the power of Energy Psychology protocols to shift psychological states and their neurological underpinnings while at the same time maintaining a deep respect for the client's inner wisdom and self-healing capacities.

References

Ardito, R. B., & Rabellino, D. (2011). Therapeutic alliance and outcome of psychotherapy: Historical excursus, measurements, and prospects for research. *Frontiers in Psychology, 2.* doi:10.3389/fpsyg.2011.00270

Association for Comprehensive Energy Psychology. (2012). Membership survey. Retrieved from https://www.energypsych.org/resource/resmgr/membership/ACEP_2012_Member_Survey.pdf

Berghash, R., & Jillson K. (1998). Thoughts on psyche, soul, and spirit. *Journal of Religion and Health, 37*, 313–322. doi:10.1023/A:1022979723704

Bordin, E. S. (1979). The generalizability of the psychoanalytic concept of the working alliance. *Psychotherapy: Theory, Research, and Practice, 16*, 252–260. doi:10.1037/h0085885

Chalmers, J. S. (2015). *An exploration of the experiences of Emotional Freedom Techniques (EFT) practitioners* (unpublished master's thesis). University of Northampton, UK. Retrieved from http://tinyurl.com/zfmyf4a

Church, D. (2013). Clinical EFT as an evidence-based practice for the treatment of psychological and physiological conditions. *Psychology, 4*(8), 645–654. doi:10.4236/psych.2013.48092

Church, D., Feinstein, D., Palmer-Hoffman, J., Stein, P. K., & Tranguch, A. (2014). Empirically supported psychological treatments: The challenge of evaluating clinical innovations. *Journal of Nervous and Mental Disease, 202*, 699–709. doi:10.1097/NMD.0000000000000188

Church, D., Stapleton, P., Mollon, P., Feinstein, D., Boath, E., Mackay, D., & Sims, R. (2018). Guidelines for the treatment of PTSD using Clinical EFT (Emotional Freedom Techniques). *Healthcare, 6*(4), 146. doi:10.3390/healthcare6040146

Church, D, Stapleton, P., & Sabot, D. (2020). App-based delivery of Clinical Emotional Freedom Techniques: Cross-sectional study of app user self-ratings. *JMIR mHealth and uHealth, 8*(10):e18545. doi:10.2196/18545

Church, D., Stern, S., Boath, E., Stewart, A., Feinstein, D., & Clond, M. (2017). Emotional Freedom Techniques to treat posttraumatic stress disorder in veterans: Review of the evidence, survey of practitioners, and proposed clinical guidelines. *Permanente Journal, 21*, 16–100. doi:10.7812/TPP/16-100

Corrigan, F. M., Fisher, J. J., & Nutt, D. J. (2011). Autonomic dysregulation and the Window of Tolerance model of the effects of complex emotional trauma. *Journal of Psychopharmacology (Oxford, England), 25*(1), 17–25. doi:10.1177/0269881109354930

Damiano, R. F., Costa, L. A., Viana, M. T., Moreira-Almeida, A., Lucchetti, A. L., & Lucchetti, G. (2016). Brazilian scientific articles on "spirituality, religion and health." *Archives of Clinical Psychiatry, 43*(1), 11–16. doi:10.1590/0101-60830000000073

Duckworth, M. P., & Follette, V. M. (Eds.). (2011). *Retraumatization: Assessment, treatment, and prevention.* New York, NY: Routledge.

Eden, D. (2008). *Energy medicine* (rev. ed.). New York, NY: Tarcher/Penguin Random House.

Feinstein, D. (2005). Practitioner impressions of . Effectiveness by diagnostic category. Retrieved from https://www.innersource.net/ep/articlespublished/allarticles/61-practitioner-impressions-of-energy-psychology.html

Feinstein, D. (2016). A survey of energy psychology practitioners: Who they are, what they do, who they help. *Energy Psychology: Theory, Research, and Treatment, 8*(1), 33–39. doi:10.9769/EPJ.2016.08.1.DF

Feinstein, D. (2019). Words to tap by: The uses of language in energy psychology protocols. *Energy Psychology: Theory, Research, and Treatment, 11*(1), 41–56. doi:10.9769/EPJ.2019.11.1.DF

Feinstein D. (2021). Six empirically-supported premises about energy psychology: Mounting evidence for a controversial therapy. *Advances in Mind-Body Medicine, 35*(2), 17–32.

Gallo, F. P. (2004). *Energy psychology: Explorations at the interface of energy, cognition, behavior, and health* (2nd ed.). New York, NY: CRC Press.

Gaudiano, B. A., Brown, L. A., & Miller, I. W. (2012). Tapping their patients' problems away?: Characteristics of psychotherapists using energy meridian techniques. *Research on Social Work Practice, 22*, 647–655. doi:10.1177/1049731512448468

Hamne, G., & Sandstrom, U. (2014). *Resolving yesterday: First aid for stress and trauma with TTT.* Scotts Valley, CA: CreateSpace.

Hartung, J., & Morales, N. (2019). Psychological and medical applications of certain innovative therapies in correctional settings: Clinician, staff, and client observations from three institutions. *Energy Psychology: Theory, Research, and Treatment, 11*(1), 57-64. doi:10.9769/EPJ.2019.11.1.JH

Heide, F. J., & Borkovec, T. D. (1984). Relaxation-induced anxiety: Mechanisms and theoretical implications. *Behaviour Research and Therapy, 22*(1), 1–12. doi:10.1016/0005-7967(84)90027-5

Kalla, M., Simmons, M., Robinson, A., & Stapleton, P. (2018). Emotional freedom techniques (EFT) as a practice for supporting chronic disease healthcare: a practitioners' perspective. *Disability and Rehabilitation, 40,* 1654–1662. doi:10.1080/09638288.2017.1306125

Kalla, M., Simmons, M., Robinson, A., Stapleton, P. (2020). Making sense of chronic disease using Emotional Freedom Techniques (EFT): An existential view of illness. *Explore, 16,* 214–224. doi:10.1016/j.explore.2020.03.006

Larson, V. A. (1987). An exploration of psychotherapeutic resonance. *Psychotherapy, 24,* 321–324. doi:10.1037/h0085722

Leskowitz, E. (2016). Integrative medicine for PTSD and TBI: Two innovative approaches. *Medical Acupuncture, 28*(4), 181–183. doi:10.1089/acu.2016.1168

Linstone, H. A., & Turoff, M. (1975). *The Delphi Method: Techniques and applications.* Reading, MA: Addison-Wesley.

Mason, E. (2012). Energy psychology and psychotherapy: A study of the use of energy psychology in psychotherapy practice. *Counselling and Psychotherapy Research, 12,* 224–232. doi:10.1080/14733145.2012.657208

May, R. (1989). *The art of counseling* (rev. ed.). New York, NY: Gardner Press. (Original work published 1939).

Mitchell, J., & Chatzidamianos, G. (2020). Emotional Freedom Techniques—how to make it mainstream; a thematic analysis of practitioners' views. *Energy Psychology: Theory, Research, & Treatment, 12*(1), 28–43. doi:10.9769/EPJ.2020.12.1.JM

Mollon, P. Client safety. (2013). In D. Church & S. Marohn (Eds.), *Clinical EFT Handbook* (Vol 2; pp. 355–362). Fulton, CA: Energy Psychology Press.

Nairn, C. A. (2020). *From the outside in: Incorporating the use of EFT into traditional psychotherapeutic approaches and its impact on therapeutic alliance* (Unpublished doctoral dissertation). University of Exeter, Exeter, UK. Retrieved from http://hdl.handle.net/10871/122720

Polster, E., & Polster, M. (1974). *Gestalt therapy integrated: Contours of theory and practice.* New York, NY: Vintage.

Rogers, C. R. (1980). *Way of being.* Boston, MA: Houghton Mifflin.

Schulz, K. (2009). Integrating energy psychology into treatment for adult survivors of childhood sexual abuse. *Energy Psychology: Theory, Research, & Treatment, 1*(1), 15–22. doi:10.9769/EPJ.2009.1.1.KS

Schwartz, R. (2021). *No bad parts: Healing trauma and restoring wholeness with the internal family systems model.* Louisville, CO: Sounds True.

Sebastian, B., & Nelms, J. (2017). The effectiveness of Emotional Freedom Techniques in the treatment of post-traumatic stress disorder: A meta-analysis. *Explore, 13*(1), 16–25. doi:10.1016/j.explore.2016.10.001

Stapleton, P. (2019). *The science behind tapping.* Carlsbad, CA: Hay House.

Stapleton, P., & Chatwin, H. (2017). Determining highly desirable traits of an effective emotional freedom techniques practitioner: A Delphi study. *Energy Psychology: Theory, Research, & Treatment, 9*(2), 13–25. doi:10.9769/EPJ.2017.9.2.PS

Stickle, M., & Arnd-Caddigan, M. (2019). *Intuition in psychotherapy: From research to practice.* New York, NY: Routledge.

Watkins, J. G. (1971). The affect bridge: A hypnoanalytic technique. *International Journal of Clinical and Experimental Hypnosis, 19*(1), 21–27. doi:10.1080/00207147108407148

White, I. C. (2015). *It helps me to love my work: An interpretative phenomenological analysis of the senior therapist experience of using energy psychology in psychotherapy for trauma* (Unpublished master's thesis). Dublin Business School (School of Arts), Dublin. Retrieved from http://hdl.handle.net/10788/2054

Wittfoth, D., Pfeiffer, A., Bohne, M., Lannfermann, H., & Wittfoth, M. (2020). Emotion regulation through bifocal processing of fear inducing and disgust inducing stimuli. *BMC Neuroscience, 21,* 47. doi:10.1186/s12868-020-00597-x

If you would like to write book reviews for Energy Psychology *journal, we'd love to hear from you. Get free inspiring books! Contact Stephanie Marohn at angel@stephaniemarohn.com*

Healing Ourselves: Biofield Science and the Future of Health

Shamini Jain, PhD

Sounds True, 2021
Hardcover, 320 pages
$24.99
ISBN: 978-1683644330

"The quality of your thoughts, beliefs and consciousness produces a profound effect in your body." That is the profound message conveyed, in clear and convincing terms, by *Healing Ourselves.* Author Shamini Jain takes us on a tour through the traditional concepts of energy healing as conceived by ancient civilizations. Remarkably, they reflect research findings now emerging from the empirical measurement of the biofield, an interface of energy and information that connects consciousness and the physical body.

Stunning case histories, such as that of two-and-a-half year old Meera who was diagnosed with an inoperable brain tumor, illustrate the power of energy healing. They demonstrate that when those invisible fields are influenced by energy modalities, even fatal diseases are sometimes cured.

Beyond dramatic remissions, *Healing Ourselves* reviews the science showing how these techniques raise our general level of well-being. Biofield effects can even extend beyond space and time, upending our conventional concepts of how the world works.

Jain points out that modern medicine has little to do with healing, focusing almost entirely on disease. The World Health Organization estimates that chronic disease accounts for three quarters of all deaths, plus an annual bill to society in the trillions of dollars. Yet despite their promise, biofield therapies have had difficulty gaining traction in mainstream settings.

One chapter of the book provides a fascinating behind-the-scenes view of how Jain conceived, designed, and conducted her first ambitious study. It sought to answer the question of whether energy healing would decrease fatigue and improve hormonal function in breast cancer survivors. While subjective measures such as well-being improved, so did objective biomarkers. Studies like this are important because they show that energy healing can affect us down to the most basic levels of cell biology. Objective physiological change accompanies subjective emotional well-being. Other studies also show that energy healing affects even serious diseases such as autoimmune and heart disease.

Jain's story also illustrates how difficult it is to get such studies approved and completed in traditional academic settings; hers was the first and last biofield study conducted at her alma mater. Skepticism, denial, and an inability to reach beyond what she calls "pathogenic thinking" hold back the study of advanced healing methods. She is mystified as to why scientific colleagues pay such little attention to this groundbreaking research when the potential impact on patients is life-changing.

The third part of the book includes practices and worksheets. These allow you to undertake your own personal exploration of the effects of biofield healing. Simple exercises based on breathing, movement, or self-reflection can raise your level of well-being and give you a "felt sense" of what biofield shifts feel like in your body.

While professionals will be intrigued by the solid science and inspiring conceptual framework in *Healing Ourselves*, this is a straight-from-the-heart book that patients and their families will find deeply meaningful as well. With the healing power of the biofield as close as our own consciousness, it is destined to become the medicine of the future.

Radical Intuition: A Revolutionary Guide to Using Your Inner Power

Kim Chestney

New World Library, 2020
Softcover, 312 pages
Price: $15.95
ISBN: 978-1608687145

Reviewed by Carol Atkinson

The holistic healing universe encourages people to rely on their intuition rather than advice gleaned from other people or resources. Even healers recount relying on their own intuition to resolve problems. For the uninitiated, knowing just exactly what intuition is—the sound of it or the information it provides—can be rather perplexing.

Kim Chestney's (2020) *Radical Intuition* brings a multifaceted approach to understanding what intuition is, what it is when it's heard, and how to get in touch with it. Out of the many definitions or explanations, the most cogent of Chestney's approaches is that when attuned to one's intuition, a person is operating at one with spirit, and when that happens, the person is living with purpose.

Radical Intuition is full of down-to-earth information about easy ways to check in with your intuition or to recognize a thought or feeling as such. The greater portion of the book reviews the meaning of intuition from different perspectives, helping the reader connect with something he or she may not have recognized in the past as intuition. Chestney suggests even asking questions about intuition (Did I listen to my intuition when attempting to solve a problem? Did I deny what information was given me?). By doing that, a person begins a relationship with it. She suggests that the more is asked of and about intuition the more it will come to meet the person and connect with her. "Your intuition is your personal translator—turning universal wisdom into personal insight" (p. 37).

Chestney writes that the role of intuition is to bring information to a person's consciousness from the inside, rather than from the outside. "Is intuition a gut feeling? Is it a knowingness? Is it a creative idea? Is it a revelation from God? The answer to all of these things is: *Yes*" (p. 33). This inside information comes to each of us from a variety of sources—feelings, thoughts, images, or nonlocal spiritual experiences.

Thus Chestney suggests that intuition comes to us from four dimensions: (a) intuitive wisdom through our body via the various physical senses, (b) through our mind via thoughts, (c) through our heart by emotions or feelings, and (d) via our spirit through spiritual experiences.

To help corral those broad categories, she suggests that each dimension can be represented by an archetype.

The physical dimension is represented by the Healer, wherein the person receives information from the body and senses. These Healer archetypes tend to have a strong connection to the earth and often support others in enhancing their physical well-being.

The dimension of the mind, which she labels the Sage or mindful intuition, is when intuitive information comes from thoughts or just plain inner knowingness. Perhaps there are flashes of insight, foresight, or some fear that is not immediately clear.

The heart dimension is represented by the Visionary archetype or creative intuition. This intuitive type tends to be very goal-oriented, seeking to improve or change circumstances to enhance his or her life. This type could be very creative, an innovator, or one who has new and unheard-of ideas.

Finally, the spiritual dimension is represented by the Mystic or transcendental intuition. This type of intuitive tends to be open to spirit's deepest secrets and may have mystical experiences. This type may also have experienced bliss or a deeply felt love for all things.

What's helpful for the book as a whole and for understanding and applying the information is an Intuition Affinity Quiz that identifies which of the four intuitive types the reader may be. Thus readers can understand the way of their personal archetype, as well as deepen their intuition with meditations or other modalities. Additionally, readers can also discover ways to improve or heighten their intuitive abilities via the other three archetypes or dimensions.

This is a book worth reading. It's clearly written and accessible. The archetype quiz, in particular, helps bridge the abstract with the physical. While it seems to be written to a broad audience interested in the topic, there is certainly application for both the practitioner and the client. Helping the client connect with her own intuition could be of higher service.

Carol Atkinson is a professor of digital media specializing in free speech, gender in the media, and personal interests in the myriad levels of consciousness. Email: atkinson@ucmo.edu

Overwhelmed and Over It: Embrace Your Power to Stay Centered and Sustained in a Chaotic World

Christine Arylo
New World Library, 2020
Softcover, 344 pages
$17.95
ISBN: 978-1608686773

Reviewed by Cary Bell Wheeler

Overwhelmed and Over It speaks to the modern-day woman by acknowledging what presumably most of us feel: burned out. You must become aware of the issue to have the ability to change it, author Christine Arylo says, and asks the reader to acknowledge the systemically created and self-generated roots of overwhelm, burnout, and self-sacrifice.

I began the book enthusiastically, nodding along in the introduction, which reads like a workbook: first citing the causes at the core of the burnout that plagues women today, and then offering a quiz to find your "Burnout Imprint."

The chapters that follow review what Arylo describes as the 12 specific imprints at the root of burnout. The 12 chapters are contained within five sections focusing on: liberating success, life force, the heart, time, and power. At the end of each chapter, she presents practices or questions to guide the reader to take the steps presented in the chapter. Within each chapter are glyphs, or images that illustrate the idea presented. The images may help the reader understand the concepts better than or differently from reading the text. I found them to be helpful, especially for Work/Life Balance, which Arylo calls a "duality reality" that isn't working.

I found the book to be educational and felt it was great for doing an internal review of where my focus and energy is currently going, but I did not finish the book with as many actionable practices as I had hoped. Suggestions like creating a morning and evening routine, daily meditation, and intentionally blocking time on your calendar are all helpful, but not new. I believe the book would best be used as a workbook or read in parts so the reader can focus on that portion and dedicate time to changing/upgrading that prior to moving on to the next chapter.

Cary Bell Wheeler works in sales but enjoys spending her free time reading and writing. She is a mom to a three-year old girl who is the light of her life. Cary and her family live in Florida and like to spend time outside. Email: bell.cary@gmail.com

Whole Body Healing: Create Your Own Path to Physical, Emotional, Energetic, and Spiritual Wellness

Emily A. Francis
Llewellyn, 2020
Softcover, 264 pages
$21.99
ISBN: 978-0738762180

Reviewed by Charles B. Crenshaw Jr.

As the cliché goes, necessity is the mother of invention, and nowhere is that more obvious than what Emily Francis relates in her inspiring book about her own healing from severe anxiety and panic and helping her daughter recover from an autism spectrum condition.

The host of a radio show related to healthy living and a trained professional in complementary healing methods, the author was thrust headlong into seeking ways and means for her and her child to be healthy and happy. The regular allopathic paradigm proved less than successful in helping with her child's condition and this spurred Francis to find a way where no way seemed possible.

It is clear to this reviewer that the author's training in modalities such as Dr. John Upledger's craniosacral therapy, lymph drainage modalities and more, as well as her yoga teacher training, has informed the contents of this book. She has done a service for people who know nothing about the paradigm the medical establishment commonly refers to as complementary or alternative.

Filled with practical exercises, *Whole Body Healing* introduces the reader to methods of relaxation and other yoga therapy practices that are useful in self-regulation. The exercises are about making you aware of the possibilities. The value in this book is in informing the average person who has been told these possibilities don't exist, or are some kind of snake oil, that the possibilities do exist. The reviewer can't make this point enough.

Francis takes the reader through a brief introduction to the body and its systems, including a very interesting table of how muscles of the body are related to emotions—a valuable piece of information. She introduces the reader to mental and emotional therapies, energetic therapies, and hands-on healing practices.

One of the most valuable things in the book is the listing and explanation of many different modalities, some of which Francis used to help her child. The information is valuable for the person searching for another way or an additional way to achieve good physical and emotional health. She informs the novice about everything from hypnosis to acupuncture and other energy modalities.

A very good introduction for someone new to the idea of holistic health.

Charles Crenshaw Jr., MS, is a lifelong meditator and meditation teacher, interfaith minister, consulting hypnotist and neuro-linguistic programming trainer, EFT practitioner, author of Pathless Path: God, Grace, Guru, *co-author of* EFT for Meditation, *and contributing author to the* Clinical EFT Handbook. *Email: charles@eliminateyourblock.com*

The effect of Emotional Freedom Techniques on nurses' stress, anxiety, and burnout levels during the COVID-19 pandemic: A randomized controlled trial

Dincer, B., & Inangil, D. (2020). The effect of Emotional Freedom Techniques on nurses' stress, anxiety, and burnout levels during the COVID-19 pandemic: A randomized controlled trial. *Explore: The Journal of Science and Healing, 17*(2), 109–114. doi:10.1016/j.explore.2020.11.012

Abstract

Background and objective: Infectious disease outbreaks pose psychological challenges to the general population, and especially to healthcare workers. Nurses who work with COVID-19 patients are particularly vulnerable to emotions such as fear and anxiety, due to fatigue, discomfort, and helplessness related to their high intensity work. This study aims to investigate the efficacy of a brief online form of Emotional Freedom Techniques (EFT) in the prevention of stress, anxiety, and burnout in nurses involved in the treatment of COVID patients.

Methods: The study is a randomized controlled trial. It complies with the guidelines prescribed by the Consolidated Standards of Reporting Trials (CONSORT) checklist. It was conducted in a COVID-19 department at a university hospital in Turkey. We recruited nurses who care for patients infected with COVID-19 and randomly allocated them into an intervention group ($n = 35$) and a no-treatment control group ($n = 37$). The intervention group received one guided online group EFT session.

Results: Reductions in stress ($p < .001$), anxiety ($p < .001$), and burnout ($p < .001$) reached high levels of statistical significance for the intervention group. The control group showed no statistically significant changes on these measures ($p > .05$).

Conclusions: A single online group EFT session reduced stress, anxiety, and burnout levels in nurses treating COVID-19.

Investigating the effect of national government physical distancing measures on depression and anxiety during the COVID-19 pandemic through meta-analysis and meta-regression

Castaldelli-Maia, J. M., Marziali, M. E., Lu, Z., & Martins, S. S. (2021). Investigating the effect of national government physical distancing measures on depression and anxiety during the COVID-19 pandemic through meta-analysis and meta-regression. *Psychological Medicine*, 1–13. doi:10.1017/S0033291721000933

Abstract

Background: COVID-19 physical distancing measures can potentially increase the likelihood of mental disorders. It is unknown whether these measures are associated with depression and anxiety.

Objectives: To investigate meta-analytic global levels of depression and anxiety during the COVID-19 pandemic and how the implementation of mitigation strategies (i.e., public transportation closures, stay-at-home orders, etc.) impacted such disorders.

Data sources: PubMed, MEDLINE, Web of Science, BIOSIS Citation Index, Current Content Connect, PsycINFO, CINAHL, medRxiv, and PsyArXiv databases for depression and anxiety prevalences; Oxford Covid-19 Government Response Tracker for the containment and closure policies indexes; Global Burden of Disease Study for previous levels of depression and anxiety.

Study eligibility criteria: Original studies conducted during COVID-19 pandemic, which assessed categorical depression and anxiety, using PHQ-9 and GAD-7 scales (cutoff > 10).

Participants and interventions: General population, healthcare providers, students, and patients. National physical distancing measures.

Study appraisal and synthesis methods: Meta-analysis and meta-regression.

Results: In total, 226,638 individuals were assessed within the 60 included studies. Global prevalence of both depression and anxiety during the COVID-19 pandemic was 24.0% and 21.3%, respectively. There were differences in the prevalence of both anxiety and depression reported across regions and countries. Asia (17.6% and 17.9%), and China (16.2% and 15.5%) especially, had the lowest prevalence of both disorders. Regarding the impact of mitigation strategies on mental health, only public transportation closures increased the prevalence of anxiety, especially in Europe.

Limitations: Country-level data on physical distancing measures and previous anxiety/depression may not necessarily reflect local (i.e., city-specific) contexts.

Conclusions and implications of key findings: Mental health concerns should not be viewed only as a delayed consequence of the COVID-19 pandemic, but also as a concurrent epidemic. Our data provide support for policymakers to consider real-time enhanced mental health services, and increase initiatives to foster positive mental health outcomes.

Positive impact of mindfulness meditation on mental health of female teachers during the COVID-19 outbreak in Italy

Matiz, A., Fabbro, F., Paschetto, A., Cantone, D., Paolone, A. R., & Crescentini, C. (2020). Positive impact of mindfulness meditation on mental health of female teachers during the COVID-19 outbreak in Italy. *International Journal of Environmental Research and Public Health, 17*(18), 6450. doi:10.3390/ijerph17186450

Abstract
The Covid-19 pandemic and subsequent public health measures were shown to impact negatively on people's mental health. In particular, women were reported to be at higher risk than men of developing symptoms of stress/anxiety/depression, and resilience was considered a key factor for positive mental health outcomes. In the present study, a sample of Italian female teachers (*n* = 66, age: 51.5 ± 7.9 years) was assessed with self-report instruments one month before and one month after the start of the Covid-19 lockdown: mindfulness skills, empathy, personality profiles, interoceptive awareness, psychological well-being, emotional distress, and burnout levels were measured. Meanwhile, they received an eight-week Mindfulness-Oriented Meditation (MOM) course, through two group meetings and six individual video-lessons. Based on baseline personality profiles, analyses of variance were performed in a low-resilience (LR, *n* = 32) and a high-resilience (HR, *n* = 26) group. The LR and HR groups differed at baseline in most of the self-report measures. Pre–post MOM significant improvements were found in both groups in anxiety, depression, affective empathy, emotional exhaustion, psychological well-being, interoceptive awareness, character traits, and mindfulness levels. Improvements in depression and psychological well-being were higher in the LR vs. HR group. We conclude that mindfulness-based training can effectively mitigate the psychological negative consequences of the Covid-19 outbreak, helping in particular to restore well-being in the most vulnerable individuals.

The breadth of confrontations as a prejudice reduction strategy

Chaney, K. E., Sanchez, D. T., Alt, N. P., & Shih, M. J. (2021). The breadth of confrontations as a prejudice reduction strategy. *Social Psychological and Personality Science, 12*(3), 314–322. doi:10.1177/1948550620919318

Abstract
Past research on prejudice confrontations as a prejudice reduction tool has only examined bias that was implicated in the confrontation, such as the use of negative Black stereotypes after being confronted for using negative Black stereotypes. Examining the breadth of prejudice confrontations, we hypothesize that confronted individuals should

subsequently use fewer negative and positive stereotypes about other racial minority groups, and fewer stereotypes about groups stigmatized along other identity dimensions (e.g., gender). In two studies, White participants confronted for the use of negative Black stereotypes used fewer negative Latino stereotypes (Study 1), positive Black, but not Asian, stereotypes and fewer gender role stereotypes (Study 2). Additionally, participants confronted for female gender role stereotypes subsequently used fewer negative Black and Latino stereotypes 24–72 hours later due to greater racial egalitarian motivation (Study 3). Thus, prejudice confrontations have a broad effect on reducing bias toward multiple stigmatized groups across identity dimensions.

Black intragroup empathic responding to police interracial violence: Effects of victim stereotypicality and blacks' racial identification

Johnson, J. D., Lecci, L., & Dovidio, J. (2020). Black intragroup empathic responding to police interracial violence: Effects of victim stereotypicality and blacks' racial identification. *Social Psychological and Personality Science, 11*(5), 579–587. doi:10.1177/1948550619859316

Abstract

Despite the public outrage in response to police violence against unarmed Black men, work on the psychological dynamics of reactions to these incidents is relatively rare. The present research examined whether empathy for a Black male victim of White police interracial violence would vary as a function of victim stereotypicality (stereotypic/counterstereotypic) and Black participant racial identity. In Study 1, 140 Black participants were recruited from Amazon Mechanical Turk (MTurk). As hypothesized, Black participants low in racial identification reported less empathy for the stereotypical relative to the counterstereotypical victim. Those high in racial identification showed relatively high levels of empathy regardless of the characteristics of the Black victim. Study 2 replicated these effects with 263 Black MTurk participants. This research highlights the value of considering individual differences in the Black observers (racial identification) and the characteristics of Black victims to better understand the psychological processes involved in intragroup responses to police violence.

Combat experience and the foreign policy positions of veterans

Endicott, T. W. (2020). Combat experience and the foreign policy positions of veterans. *Social Science Quarterly, 101*(4), 1413–1429. doi:10.1111/ssqu.12796

Abstract

Objective: Prior work on the effect of combat on veterans typically measures combat experience as a dichotomous event. I extend work in this area by theorizing and empirically accounting for the number of unique combat experiences a veteran endures and how that associates with the veteran's outlook on foreign policy.

Methods: I utilize an original survey that asks for multiple types of military combat experience, as well as foreign policy positions.

Findings: Consistent with previous research, I find that veterans tend to be more hawkish than civilians. When I account for veterans' number of unique combat experiences, however, I find that the more combat experiences veterans endure the less hawkish their foreign policy positions are. Moreover, consistent with literature from military psychology, this association only holds for veterans who express more regret about their time in the military.

Conclusions: The results should encourage public opinion scholars to consider the effects that the number of individual combat event experiences and regret have on veterans' issue positions more broadly.

Partisan gaps in political information and information-seeking behavior: Motivated reasoning or cheerleading?

Peterson, E., & Iyengar, S. (2021). Partisan gaps in political information and information-seeking behavior: Motivated reasoning or cheerleading? *American Journal of Political Science, 65*(1), 133–147. doi:10.1111/ajps.12535

Abstract

Do partisan disagreements over politically relevant facts, and preferences for the information sources from which to obtain them, represent genuine differences of opinion or insincere cheerleading? The answer to this question is crucial for understanding the scope of partisan polarization. We test between these alternatives with experiments that offer incentives for correct survey responses and allow respondents to search for information before answering each question. We find that partisan cheerleading inflates divides in factual information, but only modestly. Incentives have no impact on partisan divides in information search; these divides are no different from those that occur outside the survey context when we examine web-browsing data from the same respondents. Overall, our findings support the motivated reasoning interpretation of misinformation; partisans seek out information with congenial slant and sincerely adopt inaccurate beliefs that cast their party in a favorable light

Sharp as a Fox: Are foxnews.com visitors less politically knowledgeable?

Licari, P. R. (2020). Sharp as a fox: Are Foxnews.com visitors less politically knowledgeable? *American Politics Research, 48*(6), 792–806. doi:10.1177/1532673X20915222

Abstract

In 2012, a survey research was publicized suggesting that Fox News viewers were not only less informed than consumers of other news media but also less informed than people abstaining from news media entirely. Many have taken this to be unequivocally true and the study remains popular among political discussants to this day. However, virtually all of the investigations used to advance the argument focus on current events type knowledge and neglect important controls that could influence both political knowledge and Fox News consumption. Furthermore, no research to date has investigated any effects stemming from consuming the network's online content (i.e., from foxnews.com). This article aims to contribute these gaps. Using the 2016 American National Election Survey (ANES), I investigate whether consuming content from foxnews.com is associated with decreased political knowledge. I find no differences in knowledge concerning how the U.S. political system works (what I call process-related knowledge) but do find a significant, negative relationship between visiting foxnews.com and facts about society writ large (what I call society-oriented knowledge). These effects persist even when controlling for party, ideology, and conservative-group affinity and in the preponderance of matching procedures employed to reduce concerns of self-selection. Implications and avenues of future research are also discussed.

Would you notice if fake news changed your behavior? An experiment on the unconscious effects of disinformation

Bastick, Z. (2021). Would you notice if fake news changed your behavior? An experiment on the unconscious effects of disinformation. *Computers in Human Behavior, 116*, 106633. doi:10.1016/j.chb.2020.106633

Abstract

A growing literature is emerging on the believability and spread of disinformation, such as fake news, over social networks. However, little is known about the degree to which malicious actors can use social media to covertly affect behavior with disinformation. A lab-based randomized controlled experiment was conducted with

233 undergraduate students to investigate the behavioral effects of fake news. It was found that even short (under 5 minutes) exposure to fake news was able to significantly modify the unconscious behavior of individuals. This paper provides initial evidence that fake news can be used to covertly modify behavior. It argues that current approaches to mitigating fake news, and disinformation in general, are insufficient to protect social media users from this threat, and it highlights the implications of this for democracy. It raises the need for an urgent cross-sectoral effort to investigate, protect against, and mitigate the risks of covert, widespread, and decentralized behavior modification over online social networks.

Calling out fake online reviews through robust epistemic belief

Banerjee, S., & Chua, A. Y. (2021). Calling out fake online reviews through robust epistemic belief. *Information and Management, 58*(3), 103445. doi:10.1016/j.im.2021.103445

Abstract

Research shows that computational algorithms can classify online reviews as authentic or fake based on linguistic nuances. This study examines whether Internet users can process reviews in an algorithmic manner to discern authenticity. It also considers the role of epistemic belief—the individual trait that inherently determines one's ability to separate fact from falsehood. In an online survey, 380 participants were each exposed to three hotel reviews—some authentic, others fake. Perceived specificity was positively related to perceived review authenticity, whereas perceived exaggeration showed a negative association. Epistemic belief with respect to justification for knowing significantly moderated both the relationships.

Emotion regulation through bifocal processing of fear inducing and disgust inducing stimuli

Wittfoth, D., Pfeiffer, A., Bohne, M., Lanfermann, H., & Wittfoth, M. (2020). Emotion regulation through bifocal processing of fear inducing and disgust inducing stimuli. *BMC Neuroscience, 21*(1), 47. doi:10.1186/s12868-020-00597-x

Abstract

Background: We present first-time evidence for the immediate neural and behavioral effects of bifocal emotional processing via visualized tapping for two different types of negative emotions (fear and disgust) in a sample of healthy participants.

Results: Independent of stimulus type, neural activation in the amygdala is increased during regulation, while activation in the ventral anterior cingulate cortex is decreased. Behavioral responses, as well as lateral and medial occipital regions and the dorsolateral prefrontal cortex show differential regulatory effects with respect to stimulus type.

Conclusions: Our findings suggest that emotion regulation through bifocal processing has a neural and behavioral signature that is distinct from previously investigated emotion regulation strategies. They support theoretical models of facilitated access to and processing of emotions during bifocal processing and suggest differential neural and behavioral effects for various types of negative emotions.

First impressions count! The role of the human's emotional state on rapport established with an empathic versus neutral virtual therapist

Ranjbartabar, H., Richards, D., Bilgin, A., & Kutay, C. (2019). First impressions count! The role of the human's emotional state on rapport established with an empathic versus neutral virtual therapist. *IEEE Transactions on Affective Computing*. doi:10.1109/TAFFC.2019.2899305

Abstract
Intelligent virtual agents are being endowed with empathic behaviors to perform roles such as virtual therapists. Studies often evaluate the level of rapport established, but do not measure the therapeutic benefit and the relative advantage of empathic versus neutral behaviors. We have created two virtual (empathic/neutral) therapists. Our experiment with 63 participants consisted of one within-subjects (empathic/neutral) and one between-subjects (order) factors. Regardless of the virtual therapist used, improvements in baseline emotion were reported after the first interaction (time one) and further improvement after the second interaction (time two). Our study reveals that if the human initially expresses strong emotional feeling for a problem they are facing, rapport will be higher for the empathic therapist, and the level of rapport established at the first meeting will persist regardless of whether the second encounter used empathic or neutral dialogue. Conversely, participants experiencing low emotional feeling reported greater rapport with the neutral therapist, and that level of rapport persisted in the second encounter with the alternative therapist. This study shows that an empathic agent will not necessarily build more rapport or deliver better emotional outcomes than a neutral agent. Further studies are needed to determine when tailoring and complex behaviors are justified.

Mindfulness improves brain–computer interface performance by increasing control over neural activity in the alpha band

Stieger, J. R., Engel, S., Jiang, H., Cline, C. C., Kreitzer, M. J., & He, B. (2021). Mindfulness improves brain–computer interface performance by increasing control over neural activity in the alpha band. *Cerebral Cortex, 31*(1), 426–438. doi:10.1093/cercor/bhaa234

Abstract
Brain-computer interfaces (BCIs) are promising tools for assisting patients with paralysis, but suffer from long training times and variable user proficiency. Mind-body awareness training (MBAT) can improve BCI learning, but how it does so remains unknown. Here, we show that MBAT allows participants to learn to increase volitionally alpha band neural activity during BCI tasks that incorporate intentional rest. We trained individuals in mindfulness-based stress reduction (MBSR; a standardized MBAT intervention) and compared performance and brain activity before and after training between randomly assigned trained and untrained control groups. The MBAT group showed reliably faster learning of BCI than the control group throughout training. Alpha-band activity in electroencephalogram signals, recorded in the volitional resting state during task performance, showed a parallel increase over sessions, and predicted final BCI performance. The level of alpha-band activity during the intentional resting state correlated reliably with individuals' mindfulness practice as well as performance on a breath counting task. Collectively, these results show that MBAT modifies a specific neural signal used by BCI. MBAT, by increasing patients' control over their brain activity during rest, may increase the effectiveness of BCI in the large population who could benefit from alternatives to direct motor control.

Large effects of brief meditation intervention on EEG spectra in meditation novices

Stapleton, P., Dispenza, J., McGill, S., Sabot, D., Peach, M., & Raynor, D. (2020). Large effects of brief meditation intervention on EEG spectra in meditation novices. *IBRO Reports, 9*, 290–301. doi:10.1016/j.ibror.2020.10.006

Abstract
This study investigated the impact of a brief meditation workshop on a sample of 223 novice meditators. Participants attended a three-day workshop comprising daily guided seated meditation sessions using music without

vocals that focused on various emotional states and intentions (open focus). Based on the theory of integrative consciousness, it was hypothesized that altered states of consciousness would be experienced by participants during the meditation intervention as assessed using electroencephalogram (EEG). Brain-wave power bands patterns were measured throughout the meditation training workshop, producing a total of 5,616 EEG scans. Changes in conscious states were analyzed using pre-meditation and post-meditation session measures of delta through to gamma oscillations. Results suggested the meditation intervention had large varying effects on EEG spectra (up to 50% increase and 24% decrease), and the speed of change from pre-meditation to post-meditation state of the EEG co-spectra was significant (with 0.76 probability of entering end-meditation state within the first minute). There was a main 5% decrease in delta power (95 % HDI = [−0.07, −0.03]); a global increase in theta power of 29% (95% HDI = [0.27, 0.33]); a global increase of 16% (95% HDI = [0.13, 0.19]) in alpha power; a main effect of condition, with global beta power increasing by 17% (95% HDI = [0.15, 0.19]); and an 11% increase (95% HDI = [0.08, 0.14]) in gamma power from pre-meditation to end-meditation. Findings provided preliminary support for brief meditation in altering states of consciousness in novice meditators. Future clinical examination of meditation was recommended as an intervention for mental health conditions particularly associated with hippocampal impairments.

Yoga-enhanced cognitive behavioural therapy (Y-CBT) for anxiety management: A pilot study

Khalsa, M. K., Greiner-Ferris, J. M., Hofmann, S. G., & Khalsa, S. B. S. (2015). Yoga-enhanced cognitive behavioural therapy (Y-CBT) for anxiety management: A pilot study. *Clinical Psychology and Psychotherapy, 22*(4), 364–371. doi:10.1002/cpp.1902

Abstract

Cognitive behavioural therapy (CBT) is an effective treatment for generalized anxiety disorder, but there is still room for improvement. The aim of the present study was to examine the potential benefit of enriching CBT with kundalini yoga (Y-CBT). Participants consisted of treatment resistant clients at a community mental health clinic. A total of 32 participants enrolled in the study and 22 completed the program. After the Y-CBT intervention, pre-post comparisons showed statistically significant improvements in state and trait anxiety, depression, panic, sleep, and quality of life. Results from this preliminary study suggest that Y-CBT may have potential as a promising treatment for those suffering from generalized anxiety disorder.

Deconstructing the effects of concentration meditation practice on interference control: The roles of controlled attention and inflammatory activity

Shields, G. S., Skwara, A. C., King, B. G., Zanesco, A. P., Dhabhar, F. S., & Saron, C. D. (2020). Deconstructing the effects of concentration meditation practice on interference control: The roles of controlled attention and inflammatory activity. *Brain, Behavior, and Immunity, 89*, 256–267. doi:10.1016/j.bbi.2020.06.034

Abstract

Prior work has linked meditation practice to improvements in interference control. However, the mechanisms underlying these improvements are relatively unknown. In the context of meditation training, improvements in interference control could result either from increases in controlled attention to goal-relevant stimuli or from reductions in automatic capture by goal-irrelevant stimuli. Moreover, few studies have linked training-related changes in attention to physiological processes, such as inflammatory activity, that are thought to influence cognitive function. This study addresses these gaps by examining associations between cognitive performance and cytokines in the context of an intensive meditation retreat. Participants were randomly assigned to complete three months of meditation training first, or to serve as waitlist controls. The waitlist-control participants then later completed a separate three-month training intervention. We assessed participants' interference control with a flanker task and used computational modeling to derive component processes of controlled and automatic attention. We also collected blood samples at the beginning, middle, and end of training to quantify changes in cytokine activity. Participants who completed training evidenced better-controlled attention than waitlist controls during the first retreat intervention, and controls showed significant improvements in controlled attention when they completed their own, second retreat. Importantly, inflammatory activity was inversely associated with controlled attention during both interventions. Our results suggest that practice of concentration meditation influences interference control by enhancing controlled attention to goal-relevant task elements, and that inflammatory activity relates to individual differences in controlled attention.

Horticultural therapy reduces biomarkers of immunosenescence and inflammaging in community-dwelling older adults: A feasibility pilot randomized controlled trial

Wong, G. C. L., Ng, T. K. S., Lee, J. L., Lim, P. Y., Chua, S. K. J., Tan, C., ... & Larbi, A. (2021). Horticultural therapy reduces biomarkers of immunosenescence and inflammaging in community-dwelling older adults: A feasibility pilot randomized controlled trial. *Journals of Gerontology: Series A, 76*(2), 307–317. doi:10.1093/gerona/glaa271

Abstract

Background: With the challenges that aging populations pose to health care, interventions that facilitate alleviation of age-related morbidities are imperative. A prominent risk factor for developing age-related morbidities is immunosenescence, characterized by increased chronic low-grade inflammation, resulting in T-cell exhaustion and senescence. Contact with nature and associated physical activities have been shown to boost immunity in older adults and may be promoted in the form of horticultural therapy (HT). We aimed to examine the effects of HT on immunosenescence.

Method: We conducted a randomized controlled trial with 59 older adults assigned to either the HT intervention or waitlist control group. Older adults in the HT intervention group underwent HT intervention program over six months. Venous blood was drawn at baseline and at the third and sixth month from the commencement of this study. For participants who attended all three blood collection time points (HT: $n = 22$; waitlist: $n = 24$), flow cytometry analysis was performed on whole blood samples to evaluate the kinetics of lymphocyte subsets over the intervention period, revealing the composition of $CD4^+$ and $CD8^+$ subsets expressing exhaustion markers—CD57, CTLA4, and KLRG1. Enzyme-linked immunosorbent assays were employed to measure changes in plasma IL-6 levels.

Results: HT is associated with increased numbers of naive $CD8^+$ T cells and fewer CTLA4-expressing terminally differentiated effector $CD4^+$ and $CD8^+$ memory T cells re-expressing CD45RA (TEMRA). Furthermore, IL-6 levels were reduced during HT, and the frequencies of naive and TEMRA $CD8^+$ T cells were found to be associated with IL-6 levels.

Conclusion: HT is associated with a reduction in the levels of biomarkers that measure the extent of T-cell exhaustion and inflammaging in older adults. The positive effects of HT on T-cell exhaustion were associated with the reduction of IL-6 levels.

Endocannabinoids inhibit the induction of virulence in enteric pathogens

Ellermann, M., Pacheco, A. R., Jimenez, A. G., Russell, R. M., Cuesta, S., Kumar, A., … Sperandio, V. (2020). Endocannabinoids inhibit the induction of virulence in enteric pathogens. *Cell, 183*(3), 650–665. doi:10.1016/j.cell.2020.09.022

Abstract

Endocannabinoids are host-derived lipid hormones that fundamentally impact gastrointestinal (GI) biology. The use of cannabis and other exocannabinoids as anecdotal treatments for various GI disorders inspired the search for mechanisms by which these compounds mediate their effects, which led to the discovery of the mammalian endocannabinoid system. Dysregulated endocannabinoid signaling was linked to inflammation and the gut microbiota. However, the effects of endocannabinoids on host susceptibility to infection has not been explored. Here, we show that mice with elevated levels of the endocannabinoid 2-arachidonoyl glycerol (2-AG) are protected from enteric infection by Enterobacteriaceae pathogens. 2-AG directly modulates pathogen function by inhibiting virulence programs essential for successful infection. Furthermore, 2-AG antagonizes the bacterial receptor QseC, a histidine kinase encoded within the core Enterobacteriaceae genome that promotes the activation of pathogen-associated type three secretion systems. Taken together, our findings establish that endocannabinoids are directly sensed by bacteria and can modulate bacterial function.

A single dose of psilocybin increases synaptic density and decreases 5-HT2A receptor density in the pig brain

Raval, N. R., Johansen, A., Donovan, L. L., Ros, N. F., Ozenne, B., Hansen, H. D., & Knudsen, G. M. (2021). A single dose of psilocybin increases synaptic density and decreases 5-HT2A receptor density in the pig brain. *International Journal of Molecular Sciences, 22*(2), 835. doi:10.3390/ijms22020835

Abstract

A single dose of psilocybin, a psychedelic and serotonin 2A receptor (5-HT_{2A}R) agonist, may be associated with antidepressant effects. The mechanism behind its antidepressive action is unknown but could be linked to increased synaptogenesis and down-regulation of cerebral 5-HT_{2A}R. Here, we investigate if a single psychedelic dose of psilocybin changes synaptic vesicle protein 2A (SV2A) and 5-HT_{2A}R density in the pig brain. Twenty-four awake pigs received either 0.08 mg/kg psilocybin or saline intravenously. Twelve pigs (n = 6/intervention) were euthanized one day post-injection, while the remaining twelve pigs were euthanized seven days post-injection (n = 6/intervention). We performed autoradiography on hippocampus and prefrontal cortex (PFC) sections with [^{3}H]UCB-J (SV2A), [^{3}H]MDL100907 (5-HT_{2A}R antagonist) and [^{3}H]Cimbi-36 (5-HT_{2A}R agonist). One day post psilocybin injection, we observed 4.42% higher hippocampal SV2A density and lowered hippocampal and PFC 5-HT_{2A}R density (−15.21% to −50.19%). These differences were statistically significant in the hippocampus for all radioligands and in the PFC for [^{3}H]Cimbi-36 only. Seven days post-intervention, there was still significantly higher SV2A density in the hippocampus (+9.24%) and the PFC (+6.10%), whereas there were no longer any differences in 5-HT_{2A}R density. Our findings suggest that psilocybin causes increased persistent synaptogenesis and an acute decrease in 5-HT_{2A}R density, which may play a role in psilocybin's antidepressive effects.

Effect of acute physical exercise on motor sequence memory

Bosch, B. M., Bringard, A., Logrieco, M. G., Lauer, E., Imobersteg, N., Thomas, A., ... Igloi, K. (2020). Effect of acute physical exercise on motor sequence memory. *Scientific Reports, 10*(1), 1–13. doi:10.1038/s41598-020-72108-1

Abstract

Acute physical exercise improves memory functions by increasing neural plasticity in the hippocampus. In animals, a single session of physical exercise has been shown to boost anandamide (AEA), an endocannabinoid known to promote hippocampal plasticity. Hippocampal neuronal networks encode episodic memory representations, including the temporal organization of elements, and can thus benefit motor sequence learning. While previous work established that acute physical exercise has positive effects on declarative memory linked to hippocampal plasticity mechanisms, its influence on memory for motor sequences, and especially on neural mechanisms underlying possible effects, has been less investigated. Here we studied the impact of acute physical exercise on motor sequence learning, and its underlying neurophysiological mechanisms in humans, using a cross-over randomized within-subjects design. We measured behavior, fMRI activity, and circulating AEA levels in 15 healthy participants while they performed a serial reaction time task before and after a short period of exercise (moderate or high intensity) or rest. We show that exercise enhanced motor sequence memory, significantly for high intensity exercise and tending towards significance for moderate intensity exercise. This enhancement correlated with AEA increase, and dovetailed with local increases in caudate nucleus and hippocampus activity. These findings demonstrate that acute physical exercise promotes sequence learning, thus attesting the overarching benefit of exercise to hippocampus-related memory functions.

Measuring actual learning versus feeling of learning in response to being actively engaged in the classroom

Deslauriers, L., McCarty, L. S., Miller, K., Callaghan, K., & Kestin, G. (2019). Measuring actual learning versus feeling of learning in response to being actively engaged in the classroom. *Proceedings of the National Academy of Sciences, 116*(39), 19251–19257. doi:10.1073/pnas.1821936116

Abstract

We compared students' self-reported perception of learning with their actual learning under controlled conditions in large-enrollment introductory college physics courses taught using 1) active instruction (following best practices in the discipline) and 2) passive instruction (lectures by experienced and highly rated instructors). Both groups received identical class content and handouts, students were randomly assigned, and the instructor made no effort to persuade students of the benefit of either method. Students in active classrooms learned more (as would be expected based on prior research), but their perception of learning, while positive, was lower than that of their peers in passive environments. This suggests that attempts to evaluate instruction based on students' perceptions of learning could inadvertently promote inferior (passive) pedagogical methods. For instance, a superstar lecturer could create such a positive feeling of learning that students would choose those lectures over active learning. Most important, these results suggest that when students experience the increased cognitive effort associated with active learning, they initially take that effort to signify poorer learning. That disconnect may have a detrimental effect on students' motivation, engagement, and ability to self-regulate their own learning. Although students can, on their own, discover the increased value of being actively engaged during a semester-long course, their learning may be impaired during the initial part of the course. We discuss strategies that instructors can use, early in the semester, to improve students' response to being actively engaged in the classroom.

Natural emotion vocabularies as windows on distress and well-being

Vine, V., Boyd, R. L., & Pennebaker, J. W. (2020). Natural emotion vocabularies as windows on distress and well-being. *Nature communications, 11*(1), 4525. doi:10.1038/s41467-020-18349-0

Abstract

To date we know little about natural emotion word repertoires, and whether or how they are associated with emotional functioning. Principles from linguistics suggest that the richness or diversity of individuals' actively used emotion vocabularies may correspond with their typical emotion experiences. The current investigation measures active emotion vocabularies in participant-generated natural speech and examined their relationships to individual differences in mood, personality, and physical and emotional well-being. Study 1 analyzes stream-of-consciousness essays by 1,567 college students. Study 2 analyzes public blogs written by over 35,000 individuals. The studies yield consistent findings that emotion vocabulary richness corresponds broadly with experience. Larger negative emotion vocabularies correlate with more psychological distress and poorer physical health. Larger positive emotion vocabularies correlate with higher well-being and better physical health. Findings support theories linking language use and development with lived experience and may have future clinical implications pending further research.

Adult playfulness: An update on an understudied individual differences variable and its role in romantic life

Brauer, K., Proyer, R. T., & Chick, G. (2021). Adult playfulness: An update on an understudied individual differences variable and its role in romantic life. *Social and Personality Psychology Compass, 15*(4), e12589. doi:10.1111/spc3.12589

Abstract

There is increasing interest in the study of individual differences in playfulness in adults, the way people frame or reframe situations in a way that they are experienced as personally interesting, intellectually stimulating, and/or entertaining. In this review, we describe and discuss its role for romantic life. After a brief introduction, we will describe theoretical approaches as to why playfulness is important in romantic life (e.g., the signal theory of playfulness) and give an overview on empirical findings on assortative mating and its role in romantic relationships (e.g., for relationship satisfaction). Finally, we discuss future directions on playfulness in romantic life and singles and open research questions.

Brain-first versus body-first Parkinson's disease: A multimodal imaging case-control study

Horsager, J., Andersen, K. B., Knudsen, K., Skjærbæk, C., Fedorova, T. D., Okkels, N., ... Borghammer, P. (2020). Brain-first versus body-first Parkinson's disease: A multimodal imaging case-control study. *Brain, 143*(10), 3077–3088. doi:10.1093/brain/awaa238

Abstract

Parkinson's disease is characterized by the presence of abnormal, intraneuronal α-synuclein aggregates, which may propagate from cell-to-cell in a prion-like manner. However, it remains uncertain where the initial α-synuclein aggregates originate. We have hypothesized that Parkinson's disease comprises two subtypes. A brain-first (top-down) type, where α-synuclein pathology initially arises in the brain with secondary spreading to the peripheral autonomic nervous system; and a body-first (bottom-up) type, where the pathology originates in the enteric or peripheral autonomic nervous system and then spreads to the brain. We also hypothesized that isolated REM sleep behavior disorder (iRBD) is a prodromal phenotype for the body-first type. Using multimodal imaging, we tested the hypothesis by quantifying neuronal dysfunction in structures corresponding to Braak stages I, II, and III involvement in three distinct patient groups. We included 37 consecutive de novo patients with Parkinson's disease into this case-control PET study. Patients with Parkinson's disease were divided into 24 RBD-negative (PDRBD−) and 13 RBD-positive cases (PDRBD+) and a comparator group of 22 iRBD patients. We used 11C-donepezil PET/CT to assess cholinergic (parasympathetic) innervation, 123I-metaiodobenzylguanidine (MIBG) scintigraphy to measure cardiac sympathetic innervation, neuromelanin-sensitive MRI to measure the integrity of locus coeruleus pigmented neurons, and 18F-dihydroxyphenylalanine (FDOPA) PET to assess putaminal dopamine storage capacity. Colon volume and transit times were assessed with CT scans and radiopaque markers. Imaging data from the three groups were interrogated with ANOVA and Kruskal-Wallis tests corrected for multiple comparisons. The PDRBD− and PDRBD+ groups showed similar marked reductions in putaminal FDOPA-specific uptake, whereas two-thirds of iRBD patients had normal scans ($p < 10$-13, ANOVA). When compared to the PDRBD− patients, the PDRBD+ and iRBD patients showed reduced mean MIBG heart:mediastinum ratios ($p < 10$-5, ANOVA) and colon 11C-donepezil standard uptake values ($p = 0.008$, ANOVA). The PDRBD+ group trended towards a reduced mean MRI locus coeruleus: pons ratio compared to PDRBD− ($p = 0.07$, t-test). In comparison to the other groups, the PDRBD+ group also had enlarged colon volumes ($p < 0.001$, ANOVA) and delayed colonic transit times ($p = 0.01$, Kruskal-Wallis). The combined iRBD and PDRBD+ patient data were compatible with a body-first trajectory, characterized by initial loss of cardiac MIBG signal and 11C-colonic donepezil signal followed by loss of putaminal FDOPA uptake. In contrast, the PDRBD− data were compatible with a brain-first trajectory, characterized by primary loss of putaminal FDOPA uptake followed by a secondary loss of cardiac MIBG signal and 11C-donepezil signal. These findings support the existence of brain-first and body-first subtypes of Parkinson's disease.

Stabilization of a brain-computer interface via the alignment of low-dimensional spaces of neural activity

Degenhart, A. D., Bishop, W. E., Oby, E. R., Tyler-Kabara, E. C., Chase, S. M., Batista, A. P., & Byron, M. Y. (2020). Stabilization of a brain-computer interface via the alignment of low-dimensional spaces of neural activity. *Nature Biomedical Engineering, 4*(7), 672–685. doi:10.1038/s41551-020-0542-9

Abstract

The instability of neural recordings can render clinical brain-computer interfaces (BCIs) uncontrollable. Here, we show that the alignment of low-dimensional neural manifolds (low-dimensional spaces that describe specific correlation patterns between neurons) can be used to stabilize neural activity, thereby maintaining BCI performance in the presence of recording instabilities. We evaluated the stabilizer with non-human primates during online cursor control via intracortical BCIs in the presence of severe and abrupt recording instabilities. The stabilized BCIs recovered proficient control under different instability conditions and across multiple days. The stabilizer does not require knowledge of user intent and can outperform supervised recalibration. It stabilized BCIs even when neural activity contained little information about the direction of cursor movement. The stabilizer may be applicable to other neural interfaces and may improve the clinical viability of BCIs.

Human biofield therapy modulates tumor microenvironment and cancer stemness in mouse lung carcinoma

Yang, P., Rhea, P. R., Conway, T., Nookala, S., Hegde, V., Gagea, M., ... Cohen, L. (2020). Human biofield therapy modulates tumor microenvironment and cancer stemness in mouse lung carcinoma. *Integrative Cancer Therapies, 19*. doi:10.1177/1534735420940398

Abstract

Studies have demonstrated that purported biofield therapy emitted from humans can inhibit the proliferation of cancer cells and suppress tumor growth in various cancers. We explored the effects of biofield therapy on tumor growth in the Lewis lung carcinoma and expanded mechanistic outcomes. We found biofield therapy did not inhibit tumor growth. However, the experimental (Ex) condition exposed tumors had a significantly higher percentage of necrosis (24.4 ± 6.8%) compared with that of the Control condition (6.5 ± 2.7%; $p < .02$) and cleaved caspase-3 positive cells were almost 2.3-fold higher ($p < .05$). Similarly, tumor-infiltrating lymphocytes profiling showed that CD8+/CD45+ immune cell population was significantly increased by 2.7-fold in Ex condition ($p < .01$) whereas the number of intratumoral FoxP3+/CD4+ (T-reg cells) was 30.4% lower than that of the Control group ($p = .01$), leading to a significant 3.1-fold increase in the ratio of CD8+/T-reg cells ($p < .01$). Additionally, there was a 51% lower level of strongly stained CD68+ cells ($p < .01$), 57.9% lower level of F4/80high/CD206+ (M2 macrophages; $p < .02$) and a significant 1.8-fold increase of the ratio of M1/M2 macrophages ($p < .02$). Furthermore, Ex exposure resulted in a 15% reduction of stem cell marker CD44 and a significant 33% reduction of SOX2 compared with that of the Controls ($p < .02$). The Ex group also engaged in almost 50% less movement throughout the session than the Controls. These findings suggest that exposure to purported biofields from a human is capable of enhancing cancer cell death, in part mediated through modification of the tumor microenvironment and stemness of tumor cells in mouse Lewis lung carcinoma model. Future research should focus on defining the optimal treatment duration, replication with different biofield therapists, and exploring the mechanisms of action.

Daily microbreaks in a self-regulatory resources lens: Perceived health climate as a contextual moderator via microbreak autonomy

Kim, S., Cho, S., & Park, Y. (2021). Daily microbreaks in a self-regulatory resources lens: Perceived health climate as a contextual moderator via microbreak autonomy. *Journal of Applied Psychology*. doi:10.1037/apl0000891

Abstract

Grounded in self-regulatory resources and conservation of resources theories, the current research examines poor self-regulatory capacity as a precursor to microbreaks and their possible outcomes at work. Full-time employees completed multiple online surveys for 10 (n_1 = 779 daily observations) and 5 workdays (n_2 = 1,024 daily observations). In Study 1, multilevel path analysis results showed that on days when employees had poorer recovery at home (i.e., poor sleep quality), they experienced higher fatigue in the next morning (low self-regulatory capacity) and thus took microbreaks more frequently at work. In turn, their engagement in microbreaks was related to higher work engagement during the day and lower end-of-work fatigue. Furthermore, perceived health climate was found to moderate the path from morning fatigue to microbreaks. In Study 2, we replicated and confirmed the serial mediation paths found in Study 1 (poor sleep quality → morning fatigue → microbreaks → work engagement and end-of-work fatigue). Building on Study 1, Study 2 also identified microbreak autonomy as a mechanism by which perceived health climate moderates the path between morning fatigue and microbreaks (i.e., mediated moderation effect). Exploratory analyses discovered intriguing patterns of socialization microbreaks versus other microbreaks, providing further implications for the theoretical perspective. Overall, the findings support the theoretical resource perspective of microbreaks as an effective energy management strategy while at work.

Meta-analysis of neural systems underlying placebo analgesia from individual participant fMRI data

Zunhammer, M., Spisák, T., Wager, T. D., & Bingel, U. (2021). Meta-analysis of neural systems underlying placebo analgesia from individual participant fMRI data. *Nature Communications, 12*(1), 1–11. doi:10.1038/s41467-021-21179-3

Abstract

The brain systems underlying placebo analgesia are insufficiently understood. Here we performed a systematic, participant-level meta-analysis of experimental functional neuroimaging studies of evoked pain under stimulus-intensity-matched placebo and control conditions, encompassing 603 healthy participants from 20 (out of 28 eligible) studies. We find that placebo vs. control treatments induce small, widespread reductions in pain-related activity, particularly in regions belonging to ventral attention (including mid-insula) and somatomotor networks (including posterior insula). Behavioral placebo analgesia correlates with reduced pain-related activity in these networks and the thalamus, habenula, mid-cingulate, and supplementary motor area. Placebo-associated activity increases occur mainly in frontoparietal regions, with high between-study heterogeneity. We conclude that placebo treatments affect pain-related activity in multiple brain areas, which may reflect changes in nociception and/or other affective and decision-making processes surrounding pain. Between-study heterogeneity suggests that placebo analgesia is a multifaceted phenomenon involving multiple cerebral mechanisms that differ across studies.

CPSIA information can be obtained
at www.ICGtesting.com
Printed in the USA
BVHW090752070821
613846BV00006B/751

9 781604 151718